I know all about

AVIATION

By Frederick Jany
Illustrations by Anaïs Deville

Index

*"Make your life a dream, and
a dream a reality".*

— Antoine de Saint-Exupéry

Introduction

Flying hasn't always been a matter of course. From ancient myths to the first Chinese kites, the idea turned into experiment, then into patient science. In these pages, you'll discover how inventors tamed the air, from the Montgolfiers' balloon to the Wrights' engine, by learning to read the wind, balance an aircraft and measure every gesture.

Above all, aviation is about the interplay of forces. Lift lifts, drag brakes, weight attracts, thrust propels. You'll see how a wing profile deflects the air, why angle of attack matters, and how control surfaces pilot three axes. With simple examples, we'll link instruments, weather, maps and procedures to turn numbers into clear trajectories.

This book will also guide you through the living history of the sky. You'll meet tenacious pioneers, mail lines that have become networks, and crews who make every flight safe with checklists and teamwork. We'll talk about gliders, ultralights, helicopters and jets, not forgetting maintenance, safety and the ethics of the responsible pilot.

Finally, you'll learn how to prepare a flight like an investigator: analyze the weather, read a map, calculate weight, balance and fuel, then decide methodically. Through concrete experiences and inspiring stories, this introduction will invite you to look at the sky differently, with curiosity, precision and respect. Aviation then becomes a useful science, a disciplined and joyful adventure.

Frederick Jany

Chapter 1: The Origins of Aviation

1.1 - Dreams of flight in antiquity

From the earliest stories, many different peoples have imagined soaring through the skies. These stories don't yet describe airplanes, but they do reveal the same curiosity: how can the air carry a body heavier than itself? In the epics of Mesopotamia, in the myths of India and in ancient Greece, there are references to aerial chariots or heroes capable of crossing the clouds. Antiquity, from the great Mediterranean civilizations to imperial China, combined poetry and observation. Storytellers imagined daring journeys, while scientists began to study the nature of air, wind and birds. Detailed aircraft plans were not yet to be found, but essential intuitions were emerging: air exerts force, wind can lift, heat lightens. These ideas, sometimes hidden in legends, form the first step of a long staircase leading to the understanding of flight.

Among the Greeks, the legend of Daedalus and Icarus left its mark. Daedalus makes wings from feathers and wax, demonstrating an intuition: to fly, you need to imitate the weight-bearing surface of a bird and respect the conditions of the environment. The message is clear: ambition must be based on physical rules. Greek philosophers began to ponder the matter of air. Aristotle distinguished the elements and reflected on the movement of bodies, opening the way to the study of density and forces. Poets sang of the sky, but others observed the beating of wings, the shape of feathers, the way birds used the updrafts near cliffs. Even without equations, these descriptions sharpen the eye and invite us to measure, compare and test, step by step, the relationship between shape, speed and lift.

Further east, ancient China transformed the dream into a concrete object with the kite. Accounts credit the thinker Mozi and the craftsman Lu Ban with the manufacture of wooden birds capable of soaring, probably sophisticated kites. Contrary to myth, these machines actually fly, held by a line and guided by the wind. The military use them for signalling, estimating distances and winds, and sometimes to test the strength of ropes. The physical principle is simple to understand: the inclined canvas deflects the air, creating a lifting force that opposes the weight, while the drag is balanced by the tension of the rope. By varying the shape, tail and angle, you stabilize the kite. This serious game becomes a little school of flight, where you learn to read breezes, anticipate gusts and sense how one profile carries better than another.

Still in China, another bright idea appears with celestial lanterns, often linked to the strategist Zhuge Liang. A small fire heats the air trapped in a paper envelope, and the whole thing rises because hot air is lighter than cold air. This is a spectacular demonstration of Archimedes' thrust applied to the atmosphere. The flame doesn't propel anything: it changes the internal density, making the object float like a ship in water. This simple, visual experiment reveals that we can fly without flapping our wings, thanks solely to the difference in density. By observing the rise and fall of the air as it cooled, the ancients understood that continuous heat was needed to stay aloft. With the kite and the lantern, two dream routes open up: flight carried by the wind and flight carried by heated air.

Around the Mediterranean, scientists were experimenting with astonishing devices. Archytas of Taranto is said to have built a mechanical pigeon powered by compressed air, perhaps a gliding automaton rather than true free flight, but the idea is audacious: air can push. In Alexandria, Heron designed the éolipile, a sphere set in rotation by jets of steam, demonstrating that ejecting a fluid creates a reaction. These objects are more akin to laboratories and scientific theaters, but they teach the essential lesson: a directed flow produces a force and can lead to movement. In the hands of priest-engineers and the curious, they reveal that air and steam are not magically invisible, but substances capable of acting, pushing and turning. Dreams then gain a precious ally: small, repeatable experiments that transform wonder into usable knowledge.

All these paths of antiquity do not yet form aviation, but they do trace its mental map. Myths provided the impetus, ceremonies presented the sky as a territory to be explored, and the first machines, however modest, proved that the air obeys rules. By observing birds, holding a kite string, watching a lantern rise, the ancients learned to dialogue with the atmosphere. They understood that shape, angle and temperature change everything. This patient, inquisitive way of investigating was later passed on to medieval scientists and modern engineers. The dream of flight, born of simple stories and experiments, paved the way for future wings capable of transforming a hint of wind into an open path to infinity.

1.2 - Kites and early ideas in China

Wind, canvas and a simple string gave China one of the very first controllable flying objects: the kite. Its beginnings date back over two thousand years, and Mozi and the craftsman Lu Ban are often credited with creating "wooden birds" capable of soaring. Neither magic nor myth here: a kite is a wing held at the end of a string. Tilting the surface against the air deflects the flow and creates an upward force, while the string closes the triangle of forces and maintains balance. This simple principle has transformed a toy into an aerodynamics laboratory. By observing ascent, yawing and oscillations, the craftsmen learned to adjust the shape and angle until reliable stability was achieved. Each flight spoke volumes about the air, invisible but real. Thanks to these patient trials, the Chinese turned a poetic idea into a precise tool, the first step towards understanding flight and wings that carry.

The secret of these wings lay in their materials and construction details. Bamboo provided a light, flexible structure, easy to bend without breaking. Silk provided a strong, smooth sail, while paper, perfected under the administration of Cai Lun in the 2nd century, enabled even lighter, more economical surfaces. An adjustable bridle connected the line to the wing: moving the attachment knot changed the angle of attack, and thus lift and drag. The tail added at the rear lowered the center of pressure and dampened yawing. Some frames incorporated a slight curvature, which cambered the sail and increased its finesse, the balance between lift and friction. Craftsmen experimented constantly: a yard that was too rigid vibrated, while one that was too supple bent in gusts; a sail that was too taut stalled suddenly, while one that was too loose undulated and lost its lift. By dint of meticulous adjustments, practice produced simple rules that were easy to transmit and reproduce.

Chinese kites weren't just for play. Strategists used them to transmit signals visible at great distances, to test the strength and direction of the wind before an operation, or to estimate distances by unwinding a known length of line. They also knew how to observe the tension of the line to sense air layers and choose the right moment.

Some models carried bamboo whistles; the air made them sing, transforming the breeze into a sound message. Others carried ribbons, written messages or small lanterns that could be seen at dusk. Fishermen sometimes used a kite to draw a light line out to sea without a boat. Each use reinforced observation: counting string steps, noting gusts of wind, comparing two shapes thrown one after the other. In this way, the kite became at once a measuring tool, a means of communication and a school of patience, where the eye trained itself to read the air like a living map.

Alongside kites, another brilliant idea has taken off: the celestial lantern, often associated with the strategist Zhuge Liang. You can see how it works at a glance. A flame heats the air enclosed in a paper envelope; this air becomes less dense than the surrounding air and the whole thing floats, just as a boat lifts off the water. Unlike a kite, there are no lines: thrust comes from the difference in density, and stability depends on the shape of the envelope and the regularity of the flame. By observing the ascent and descent of the flame as the air cools, we can deduce that a continuous supply of heat is required to keep the flame aloft. This simple demonstration reveals Archimedes' buoyancy applied to the atmosphere, and offers a second path to the sky: instead of deflecting the wind with a wing, we lighten the interior to float. Two principles, the same curiosity: to understand how the air carries and how to navigate it safely.

Kite flying has sharpened our sense of stability. If the bridle was too short, the kite would sting and spiral; if it was too long, the kite would stall in fits and starts. Slightly bending the yardarm increased camber and thus lift, but drag had to be kept in check. Segmented models, known as "centipedes", distributed the forces over a column of rings and scales, which smoothed out movements in gusts. The dragon, swallow and hawk shapes were not purely decorative: stretched wings gave better glide, multiple tails stabilized yaw, and small gills evacuated excess pressure. Some frames featured a discreet dihedral between the two wing halves, adding an automatic return to the horizontal. All this meant mastering three quantities: lift, drag and moment. Without a written formula, the hand and eye added it all up, until a calm flight was obtained, capable of climbing high without bringing the line back in uncontrollable zigzags.

Little by little, this wind culture built a foundation of clear ideas. A wing carries thanks to its inclination and shape; a tail stabilizes; a light material helps climbing; careful measurement makes tests comparable. These practical rules circulated with the objects themselves, passing from workshop to workshop, then traveling along trade routes. Much later, other curious people, in Asia as elsewhere, would also use kites to test profiles and feel the limit of stall. What counts here is not a famous name, but a method: observe, change a single parameter, note the result, repeat. The Chinese kite has thus transformed a dream into a process, and a fickle breeze into a demanding teacher. With each successful takeoff, he reminded us that we can tame the air with patience and precision, right up to the point of imagining bigger wings. The aerial adventure begins with this thread stretched between hand and sky, the promise of even bolder explorations.

1.3 - Leonardo da Vinci and his flying machines

Italian Renaissance genius Leonardo da Vinci was undoubtedly one of the first to envisage human flight in a scientific, almost modern way. Although his flying machines never took to the air during his lifetime, his drawings and sketches bear witness to a bold vision and profound reflection on the principles of flight. Leonardo didn't just dream of flying; he observed, analyzed and sought ways to translate his observations of nature into technical solutions.

One of Leonardo's most famous sketches is that of the "propeller aircraft", a device closely reminiscent of the appearance of a modern helicopter. He imagined a large wooden screw, mounted on an axle, which would have been turned to "split" the air and create lift. His idea, though unable to work at the time due to limited materials and the absence of powerful engines, was nonetheless based on a sound principle: to fly, you had to generate sufficient upward force to overcome weight. Leonardo's propeller is a striking example of innovation, showing the intuition of an aerodynamic form which, over 400 years later, would become fundamental to the propulsion of modern airplanes and helicopters.

But Leonardo didn't limit himself to the propeller. He also designed machines that imitated birds, another symbol of flight. Among these sketches was an "ornithopter", a machine with flapping wings, intended to imitate the flapping of birds' wings. While studying birds, Leonardo had observed their graceful movement in the air and sought to reproduce this propulsion mechanism. He envisioned wings made of canvas stretched over wooden bones, with a complex system of ropes and pulleys enabling the wings to flap. Although this invention was over-ambitious and ill-suited to the physics of the time, it demonstrates Leonardo's pioneering spirit and belief in the power of engineering to overcome natural laws.

Leonardo also observed birds to understand aerodynamics and lift. In his notebooks, he took detailed notes on how birds control their flight. He noted that birds don't simply fly by flapping their wings, but also use subtle techniques, such as adjusting the angle of their wings to suit wind conditions. These observations, still primitive, already made the link between animal flight and engineering. It was with this scientific curiosity that he sought to apply the principles of nature to the machine. Other inventions of Leonardo's, such as his parachute, also bear witness to his pioneering genius: a large pyramid-shaped canvas, which he believed would stop a free fall. Although his parachute was untested in his day, it worked on principles we still use today.

But Leonardo da Vinci didn't just design machines: he sought to understand the nature of flight by studying birds and conducting experiments. For example, he observed birds gliding, and realized that this effortless flight was due to a perfect mastery of air and thermal currents. The idea of lift, which would come later in the theory of flight, was present in his mind, albeit empirically. Leonardo realized that flight depended on the balance between thrust generated by the wing and drag, as well as on interaction with the surrounding air. He was fascinated by the way in which air could be manipulated, an obsession that would lead him to draw up plans for machines that, in essence, exploited these natural forces.

Leonardo also studied concepts such as air resistance. He experimented with the shape of wings and surfaces to make the machine more efficient. This was thinking far ahead of his time, at a time when aerodynamics didn't even exist as a scientific discipline. His sketches were not simply fantastic visions, but precise studies of physical forces, materials and mechanical concepts that would prove essential for future generations.

By analyzing the way birds change angle in flight, or how they manage air turbulence, Leonardo da Vinci laid the foundations of aerodynamics. Although his work did not result in a functional flying machine, it did lay the foundations for a human flight architecture based on observation and experimentation. The principles he deduced, long before the invention of combustion engines and modern materials, would be revisited centuries later by pioneers like the Wright brothers.

Leonardo's inventions are thus a demonstration that, even if the technology of his day did not allow him to realize his dreams, his visionary spirit paved the way for generations of engineers and aviators. His machines may not have taken flight, but they enabled the science of aerodynamics to take root and grow. Even today, Leonardo da Vinci is celebrated as one of the greatest precursors of aviation, not only for his ability to imagine machines, but also for his method: observing nature, experimenting and thinking outside the limits imposed by the technology of the day.

1.4 - The Montgolfier brothers' balloons

Aviation took a decisive turn in the 18th century with the experiments of brothers Joseph-Michel and Jacques-Étienne Montgolfier. These two French inventors flew the first hot-air balloon, marking the dawn of the aerial age. Long before motorized aircraft or even airships, it was hot air, lighter than cold air, that enabled man to defy gravity. This principle, already known to the Chinese with their celestial lanterns, was to change forever the way we think about flight.

The story of the Montgolfiers began in 1782, when they set out to study hot-air propulsion. Their discovery was no accident, but the result of a series of meticulous experiments and observations. Joseph-Michel, the elder of the two, was passionate about science and physics. He observed the properties of hot air, notably that it rises naturally when heated. Inspired by this idea, he designed a device capable of exploiting this temperature difference to produce an ascent.

The first trials took place in the Vidalon region, where the Montgolfier brothers experimented with a simple balloon made of light canvas, paper and cotton cloth, which they heated with a wood fire placed beneath it. From the very first attempt, the object took shape and rose into the air. However, these first attempts were far from perfect. The balloon had not yet been mastered, but the experiment demonstrated that hot air could indeed lift a mass, even if controlling the flight remained a challenge.

On June 4, 1783, the Montgolfier brothers made their first public flight in Annonay, in the south of France, with an impressively large balloon. Measuring over 10 meters in height and 7 meters in diameter, the balloon soared to a height of 1,600 meters, covering a distance of almost 3 kilometers. It's a spectacular success, attracting the attention of both the public and the authorities. However, a crucial question remained: how to maintain this flight and prevent the balloon from falling back down again immediately after reaching its maximum altitude? The Montgolfier brothers still had no answer to this question.

In June 1783, the Montgolfier brothers made their first flight with a live passenger: a sheep, a rooster and a duck. These animals were chosen to test the impact of ascent on living beings before sending a human being on board. The balloon, which floats on hot air, flies without a motor, simply carried along by the heat. Although the flight was short, it was a decisive step towards demonstrating that man could, in theory, travel through the air. The choice of animals as passengers was not only a matter of prudence, but also of scientific curiosity: the brothers wanted to observe the effects of flight on living organisms before attempting the human experiment.

The Montgolfier brothers' success did not stop at Annonay. On November 21, 1783, the first human beings ascended in a Montgolfier balloon. On that day, Jean-François Pilâtre de Rozier, a physics professor, and François Laurent d'Arlandes, a marquis, became the first men to fly in a balloon, this time in Paris. The more sophisticated balloon is almost 12 meters high and has a closed compartment where the two men can sit. The flight lasts around 25 minutes and reaches an altitude of 900 meters. The flight, though relatively short, was a triumph. It showed that man could finally escape gravity and explore the sky. It also symbolized the beginning of modern aviation.

One of the Montgolfiers' major challenges was to control the duration and direction of the flight. Indeed, a hot-air balloon, although capable of soaring, is not easy to control. Unlike modern aircraft, which use engines to steer their trajectory, early balloons had no efficient means of navigation. Wind direction was therefore essential in determining where the balloon would land. As a result, early flights were unpredictable, adding to the excitement and danger of this new form of travel.

Nevertheless, the Montgolfier brothers didn't stop there. They continued to perfect their balloons, increasing their size and capacity. These hot-air balloons were an important first step, but the real revolution was yet to come. After their first successful demonstrations, many inventors and scientists, influenced by the Montgolfiers' success, sought to improve flight technology and make it more practical. More sophisticated balloons, with improved means of propulsion and control, saw the light of day.

Although the Montgolfier brothers did not see their invention revolutionize the world as they had hoped, they did lay the foundations for aviation. Their hot-air balloons paved the way for dirigibles, modern hot-air balloons and, ultimately, heavier-than-air machines. Thanks to their vision and perseverance, the Montgolfiers proved that it was possible for man to take to the skies. This was just the beginning of an aerial adventure that was to see dazzling developments in the centuries to come.

The Montgolfier brothers' balloons will forever go down in the history of aeronautics as a milestone in the conquest of the skies. Their exploits marked the beginning of air exploration, and inspired generations of engineers and dreamers to push the limits of what was possible even further.

1.5 - Cayley and Lilienthal gliders

After the first attempts with balloons and mechanical experiments, human flight took a crucial turn with the appearance of gliders. These engineless machines are based on aerodynamic principles that allow an aircraft to glide on air. In the 19th century, two pioneers paved the way for modern aviation with their work on gliders: Sir George Cayley and Otto Lilienthal.

Sir George Cayley, a British engineer and scientist, is often referred to as the "father of aeronautics". In the early 19th century, he began to experiment seriously with flight and to formulate theories on lift. Cayley first recognized the four essential forces of flight: lift, drag, thrust and weight. It was he who, around 1799, drew the first plans for an aircraft, a glider, with a fixed wing and an aerodynamic structure that prefigured modern aircraft.

His work was not limited to theory: Cayley built a first scale model of his glider, which he tested in 1804. This first test was rudimentary, but marked a decisive step forward. In 1853, he carried out a more advanced demonstration with a larger model, capable of carrying a person. This glider, though limited, was one of the first to take the shape of a true modern aircraft. It didn't fly as far as Cayley had hoped, but it already established a design principle that would influence all subsequent inventors. Cayley was one of the first to understand that, for an aircraft to take off and fly efficiently, it needed a sufficiently large lifting surface and a balance of forces. He also devised a rudder system to direct flight, a key idea that would be put into practice by his successors.

While Cayley laid the foundations for the design of an efficient glider, it was Otto Lilienthal in Germany who took the idea much further. At the end of the 19th century, Lilienthal carried out controlled flights with fixed-wing gliders, which he designed and built himself. The German engineer and inventor became famous for his daring experiments: between 1891 and 1896, he made over 2,000 flights with various glider models. Lilienthal was the first to give public and scientific demonstrations of controlled flight over significant distances. He was also one of the first to systematically study the principles of aircraft stability and control. His gliders are designed to allow a man to sit in them and control movement by using his body as a means of steering, modifying the angle of inclination of the wing with his weight.

Lilienthal's experimental approach was highly methodical: he took precise measurements, analyzed the results of his flights and constantly modified his designs to improve the performance of his machines. He designed several types of glider, each more efficient than the last. His light, flexible-wing gliders were well suited to the flying conditions of the time, and Lilienthal was the first to achieve significant results in controlled flight. His experiments, particularly with slope flight, where he launched himself from a hill and glided through the air, made him one of the most respected pioneers in aviation history.

Lilienthal's glider is a model of simplicity and efficiency: a large fixed wing, a light fuselage and a stabilizing, bird-like tail. The big difference with early attempts is that control movements are taken into account. By tilting his body, the pilot can steer the aircraft, modifying its flight angle to adjust direction and stability. This control system, which resembles the movements made by a bird in flight, is the first real approach to active flight control, which was later perfected in motorized aircraft.

Lilienthal's successes were a great step forward, but they were not without danger. On August 9, 1896, while flying a glider on a slope, Lilienthal met with a fatal accident. He lost control of his glider and fell to the ground. Although tragic, this accident did not overshadow the importance of his work. His experiments paved the way for understanding aircraft lift, control and stability. Lilienthal proved that human flight was not only possible, but could be mastered with the right knowledge of aerodynamics.

The work of Cayley and Lilienthal had a considerable influence on future developments in aviation. While Cayley laid the theoretical foundations of aeronautics, Lilienthal showed that controlled flight was feasible, and that engineering could solve the technical challenges associated with air control. Their direct contribution to the design of more sophisticated aircraft would be felt throughout the twentieth century, most notably in the work of the Wright brothers, who drew inspiration from their studies to create the first powered aircraft.

Cayley's and Lilienthal's gliders not only marked a turning point in the history of aviation, but also made it possible to understand and improve the mechanics of flight. Thanks to their determination, ingenuity and discoveries, these two pioneers ushered in a new era in aviation, laying the foundations for what would become one of the greatest technical advances in human history: powered flight.

Chapter 2: The Conquest of the Motorized Sky

2.1 - The Wright brothers and the Flyer 1903

The history of aviation took a decisive turn at the beginning of the 20th century with the brothers Orville and Wilbur Wright. These two American inventors were the first to achieve controlled powered flight, marking the birth of modern aviation. Their machine, the Flyer, was a technical feat that surpassed anything achieved before them. But behind this success lay years of research, trial, error and daring innovation.

The Wright brothers were not trained engineers, but aviation enthusiasts, initially interested in bird flight and the principles of controlled flight. Their journey began in 1899, when they decided to solve an as-yet unanswered problem: how to fly a heavier-than-air aircraft and control its movement through the air. At the time, many inventors had already attempted this feat, but they all failed to make their aircraft truly controllable or to achieve sustained flight. What the Wright brothers brought to the table was a deeper understanding of aerodynamics and the need to control not only lift, but also steering and stability.

The Wright's first major advance was the design of an effective control surface to steer the aircraft. Rather than relying on traditional control surfaces, such as those used on Lilienthal gliders, the Wright brothers devised a steering system using the wings themselves, making them deform to offer greater control. This innovative concept, which they called the "aileron", maintained the aircraft's balance in flight, reacting actively to changes in direction. This system would become one of the pillars of modern aircraft stability.

In 1900, they went to Kitty Hawk, a beach in North Carolina known for its strong, constant winds, an ideal place to experiment with their aircraft. For three years, the Wright brothers conducted a series of trials with gliders, testing different designs and refining their understanding of aerodynamics. In particular, they concentrated on creating a wing that could produce sufficient lift while being stable and controllable. No detail was overlooked: every aspect, from the angle of attack of the wings to the shape of the fuselage, was precisely adjusted and tested.

In 1903, they finally realized their dream. After several prototypes and numerous improvements, the Wright brothers were ready to test their Flyer, a powered aircraft capable of sustained flight. The Flyer is a wooden biplane, powered by two 12-horsepower gasoline engines, capable of propelling the aircraft to a speed of around 48 km/h. With its 12-meter wingspan and lightweight fuselage, the Flyer is a blend of clever engineering and careful construction.

On December 17, 1903, at Kitty Hawk, the Flyer's first flight finally took shape. Orville Wright took to the airplane and, after a short 36.5-meter takeoff, flew for 12 seconds, reaching an altitude of 3 meters. The flight, though brief, was historic: it was the first controlled and sustained powered flight of a heavier-than-air aircraft. This success was immediately followed by three more flights by Wilbur and Orville, confirming that sustained, controlled flight was possible.

The fourth flight of the day was the most impressive: Wilbur Wright flew the Flyer 260 meters in 59 seconds, proving that flight control was not just a fluke, but a solid, reproducible technical achievement. This moment marked the birth of modern aviation, as for the first time a powered aircraft flew in a stable, controlled and sustained manner.

However, the Flyer's success would not have been possible without the many technical adjustments and innovations made by the Wright brothers. One of their main contributions was the design of a three-axis control system, which allowed control of pitch (the aircraft's elevation or descent), roll (rotation around the longitudinal axis) and yaw (the aircraft's direction). This system was to become the standard for all future aircraft, transforming powered flight from a mere experiment into a genuine technology.

The Wright brothers were not content with their initial success. From 1904 onwards, they continued to perfect their aircraft, increasing flight capacity and improving stability. They understood that the key to making aviation practical and reliable was to solve the problems of control, stability and power. In 1905, they created a more powerful aircraft, the Flyer III, which managed to fly for over 30 minutes, setting a new record. This steady progress paved the way for commercial and military aviation, enabling aircraft to play a fundamental role in the modern world.

Despite their breakthrough, the Wright brothers did not immediately receive the recognition they deserved. Many other inventors, notably the French Voisin brothers and the German pioneers, claimed similar successes. It was not until many years later that the Wright brothers were fully recognized as the inventors of the first practical airplane. Yet their work was essential to the rise of aviation, for they showed that human flight was not just a distant dream, but a scientific and technical reality.

The Wright brothers laid the foundations of modern aviation. Their research into lift, stability and control transformed a theoretical concept into a viable technology, paving the way for faster, safer and more efficient aircraft. Thanks to their determination, vision and innovation, aviation entered a new era, marked by commercial, military and leisure flight. The Flyer of 1903 remains a symbol of this revolution, the beginning of an aviation adventure that would transform the world forever.

2.2 - The first efficient engines and propellers

At the beginning of the 20th century, it was no longer enough to get an aircraft off the ground: it had to be kept aloft, longer, further and safer. The central challenge was weight/power ratio, i.e. getting a lot of energy out of very little mass. Steam offered power, but boilers were heavy and slow. The internal combustion engine changed all that: an air-gasoline mixture ignites in a cylinder, pushes a piston, turns a crankshaft and then a propeller. This system was compact, repairable and adaptable. To lighten the load, we experimented with aluminum crankcases, simple lubrication and magneto ignition, a "dynamo" that produces the spark without a battery. Tanks remained small to keep weight down, and mechanics learned to tune carburetors and valves like tuning an instrument. Little by little, power climbed, weight dropped, and the airplane found its winning combination: a reliable engine combined with a well-designed propeller.

The Wright brothers understood the need for control as well as power. With their mechanic Charlie Taylor, they built a simple, lightweight four-cylinder gasoline engine, tailor-made for their biplane. Their real stroke of genius was the propeller: they treated it like a spinning wing. They sculpted blades with a load-bearing profile and gradually twisted them to maintain an effective angle of attack from hub to tip. By driving two counter-rotating propellers, they limited the torque that destabilizes the aircraft. This approach, based on tests, calculations and measurements, transformed a board that stirs the air into a machine that "deflects" it cleanly. The result: more thrust for the same power, shorter take-offs and smoother flights. Their method was already showing the way: intelligent form counts as much as engine power.

In Europe, Léon Levavasseur impressed with his Antoinette engines, fine liquid-cooled V8s. The V-shaped architecture offered power in a narrow, streamlined block, while water maintained an even temperature to preserve parts. These engines powered elegant aircraft, entrusted to pioneers like Hubert Latham. In another style, Alessandro Anzani launched an ingenious three-cylinder fan engine: simple, robust and relatively light. Louis Blériot used a version to cross the English Channel in 1909, proving that a modest but reliable engine is enough when it drives a well-chosen propeller. Carburetors became more stable, magnetos more regular, and valves better cooled. We learned to listen for a clatter, to feel a loss of rpm, to dose the mixture. Each improvement gained a few minutes of flight, a few meters of climb, and above all the confidence to leave the ground without hesitation.

Another family of engines quickly won over the pioneers: rotary engines, such as the Gnome, Le Rhône or Clerget. Here, it's not just the shaft that turns, but the whole motor around the fixed shaft. This results in excellent cooling, making for a very light construction and a remarkable power-to-weight ratio. The mechanics remain simple, with few heavy accessories, which facilitates maintenance. But there are trade-offs: high fuel consumption, castor oil lubrication that clogs up, and a strong gyroscopic effect that can influence cornering. Pilots learned to cope with these peculiarities, taking advantage of the liveliness of these engines to take off short and climb fast. This solution prevailed for several years, because it responded to the urgent need for power without weighing down the airframe. It also showed that every technical advance must be accompanied by precise training in flight behavior.

While engine manufacturers were making progress, propellers became veritable pieces of technical goldsmithery. Craftsmen would assemble glued wooden strips to form light, strong laminated blades, then carve them with a calculated pitch and twist. The famous Chauvière "Intégrale" illustrated this quest for efficiency: polished surface, perfect balance, clean leading edge. Pitch" is understood as the theoretical distance covered in one revolution in a perfect solid; in the air, a little is lost, but a well-designed propeller loses less. Torsion is used to maintain a consistent angle of attack along the blade, as the tip rotates faster than the base. Profiles were tested, thrust measured on benches, and the slightest vibration noted. So, the same power translated into more traction, less noise, and sharper climbs.

As engines and propellers were refined, the whole aircraft ecosystem matured. Magnetos became more reliable, carburetors more stable despite altitude, radiators better designed, and exhausts directed to limit losses. Flights became longer, climbs more vigorous, and crossing straits, skirting coastlines and flying around terrain became realistic. There's nothing magical about it: a method, tests, notebooks full of figures, wood and metal shavings on the ground. A well-tuned engine, a well-balanced propeller and a clean airframe are a winning trio. This alliance enabled pilots to aim higher and farther, and engineers to design faster, safer aircraft. With each turn of the propeller, aviation matured, transforming a fragile promise into a solid, ambitious adventure.

2.3 - Santos-Dumont and the Paris boom

Alberto Santos-Dumont, a young Brazilian fascinated by mechanics, chose Paris to tame the skies. The capital bubbled with experiments, competitions and newspapers eager for measured feats. In his workshops and hangars near the Bois de Boulogne, he assembled light, streamlined aircraft that he piloted himself. Unlike hidden scientists, he flew in broad daylight, over avenues and parks. His airships, thin "cigars" filled with hydrogen, glide at low altitude, greeted by the crowd. Santos-Dumont doesn't just want to amaze: he wants to prove that it's possible to steer a machine through the air with precision. Each outing becomes a public, timed experiment in which heading, speed and turning radius are recorded. This way of showing, measuring and repeating turns Paris into an open-air laboratory. A veritable ecosystem of manufacturers, mechanics and reporters grew up around him. The nascent world of aviation took on the allure of sport, science and spectacle combined.

His airships were numbered from n°1 to n°6, each one correcting the weaknesses of the previous one. The principle was clear: a hydrogen-filled envelope provided lift, internal balloons adjusted the shape, and a small gasoline engine turned a propeller. A lightweight keel, made of bamboo or aluminum, serves as the backbone, supporting the nacelle, tanks and controls. A rudder and centerboard keep it on course, while weight and pitch help it climb. Santos-Dumont chose ultralight materials and embraced the idea of rapid iteration: fly, note, modify. He takes off early, when the air is calm, follows the Seine to spot breezes, then returns to the hangar to measure wear and leaks. Every gram gained becomes extra meters. Every vibration tracked turns into minutes of reliability. This concern for optimization, observable by all, shows that regular aerial navigation is possible, provided that precise tuning and pilot-engineer discipline are applied.

The great Parisian challenge is called "Prix Deutsch de la Meurthe". Departing from the Parc de Saint-Cloud, flying around the Eiffel Tower and back, all in less than thirty minutes, shows that an aircraft doesn't just sway in the wind: it sails. After several attempts, Santos-Dumont achieved the feat on October 19, 1901 with his n°6, in 29 minutes 30 seconds. Official chronometers, witnesses, distances: everything was measured and confirmed, and the crowd rejoiced. Victory means more than just a medal. It proves to a huge audience that a lighter-than-air machine can follow a set route, complete a loop and return to the starting point. The pilot shares the prize money between his team and charities, boosting his popularity. Paris discovered that aviation was more than just a feat, it required rules, reference points and a sporting spirit. Fascinated, the newspapers multiplied the number of diagrams and popularizations, further accelerating the technical boom and the collective understanding of flight.

After airships, Santos-Dumont attempted the "heavier than air" adventure. His 14-bis biplane, built with box-section lifting surfaces and a simple chassis, took off publicly at Bagatelle. On October 23, 1906, under the supervision of the Aéro-Club de France, the aircraft covered a distance of around sixty meters at a few meters altitude. On

November 12, after modifications - including stabilizing lateral surfaces - it made a flight of around 220 meters, winning the Archdeacon prize for a flight of one hundred meters. What's important, for spectators and judges alike, is the method: open field, posted rules, measuring instruments, independent witnesses. These criteria give these flights a founding value in Europe, where the event is seen, filmed and timed. In the public mind, the airplane became a concrete object whose wingspan, speed and distance could be described, rather than a distant legend. Once again, Paris served as a stage and a school, linking invention, sport and certification.

Still driven by the idea of simplification, Santos-Dumont then set his sights on a tiny monoplane, the "Demoiselle". Bamboo, canvas, light engine: all aimed at minimum weight for short but fast flights, sometimes exceeding 80 to 90 km/h. He published plans and encouraged free reproduction, which inspired amateur builders and flying schools. Around him, Paris also invented new uses: helmets, goggles, suits, mobile tools in hangars. His friendship with Louis Cartier brought a practical detail that became famous: a wristwatch designed in 1904 to tell the time in flight without taking your hands off the controls. Aviation thus intersected with engineering, industry and even design. Exhibitions, demonstrations and technical articles were the order of the day; propellers, engines and wing profiles were compared, and centering and strength of materials were discussed. This ferment transforms curiosity into an industry, and an industry into a culture, accessible to the curious as well as experienced engineers.

The Paris boom, led by Santos-Dumont, established reflexes that would guide all of aviation: visibility of tests, clear rules, public measures, sharing of knowledge. The airfields of Bagatelle, Saint-Cloud and Issy-les-Moulineaux became open-air classrooms. Here, we learn that air is traded by the grams gained, the profiles better drawn, the gestures reproducible. Clubs draft rules, mechanics create methods, pilots adopt discipline. Thanks to these habits, invention leaves the solitary workshop to join a community capable of testing, comparing and progressing together. In this adventure, Santos-Dumont shines above all in his technical generosity: he shows, explains, simplifies, and makes people want to try. The youngsters see that a flying machine is not a mystery, but the sum of lucid choices. With Paris as a stage and the eyes of the public as a barometer, aviation moves from dream to profession. It is this way of learning in flight that will open the next chapters of the sky.

2.4 - From aeroplanes to rugged biplanes

At the turn of the century, from 1908 to 1914, the homebuilt aeroplane became a real system, and the biplane form became the norm. Two wings stacked one on top of the other provided a large load-bearing surface without excessively lengthening the spars. Connected by masts and shrouds, they form a highly rigid lattice frame for moderate weight. This architecture distributes bending and torsional forces more evenly, reassuring pilots and mechanics alike. In France, the Voisin brothers delivered solid airframes to Henri Farman, who began flying regularly; in the UK, the Bristol Boxkite proved the simplicity of this design. The community learns fast: wing angles are standardized, take-off speeds are recorded and settings are documented. Because it is more forgiving of errors and accepts grass runways, the biplane configuration becomes the school of the sky. The aim is not extreme speed, but consistency, stability and repairability. This trio, accessible and reliable, transforms the idea of the "aeroplane" into a robust, reproducible machine.

Robustness comes as much from the materials as from the design. Spruce stringers combine lightness and elasticity, while ash reinforces where loads are concentrated. Steel cables, criss-crossed in an X pattern between slender masts, lock in the geometry. The wing is covered in linen and tensioned by coatings that make it smooth, watertight and resistant. Between the two wings, the "bays" form easy-to-inspect frames; the central section, held by a "hut", neatly connects the airframe to the upper plane. Mechanics learn the art of "rigging": adjusting incidence, checking alignment, carefully tensioning the shrouds. A wing that's too loose wavers and loses lift; one that's too taut works poorly in gusts. It's all about balance. The craftsmen also take care of the connections between wing and fuselage, profile the masts and protect the canvas with varnish. Every gram saved and every vibration avoided translates into metres gained on take-off and minutes of untroubled flight.

On the control side, a decisive step was taken to replace the wing warp with articulated ailerons. The Wright Flyer twisted its wings; Farman, Curtiss and others adopted dedicated control surfaces, sharper and less fatiguing for the structure. The classic trio took hold: rudder, elevator and ailerons, each controlling a precise axis. Biplanes receive a fixed tailplane balanced by a rudder, sometimes with a slight dihedral for a natural lateral return. The landing gear has also evolved: two wheels, skids and bungee-corded axles to absorb shocks on grassy terrain. The aim is clear: to give the pilot reproducible gestures, a plane that responds without surprise and is forgiving. Control cables are neatly guided, pulleys aligned and tensions controlled. With these refinements, the biplane holds its trajectory better, maintains its approach speed and lands short - essential qualities for increasing test flights, training students and validating technical progress.

The biplane structure was well suited to the engines of the time. Gnome, Le Rhône and Clerget rotary engines offered an attractive power-to-weight ratio for light airframes; in-line and star engines completed the range. Avro 504s, Curtiss JN-4 "Jenny", Farman F.40s, Nieuport 17s and SPAD VIIs show that it's possible to reconcile docility, robustness and low-speed performance. These aircraft can handle long-chord wings, reduced approach speeds and rapid field repairs. They are used for training, liaison, aerial photography and the first postal lines, where ease of maintenance is appreciated. The workshops know how to glue a stick, re-tension a canopy and straighten a mast. Pilots learn to listen to engine speed, read shroud tension and feel for stability. Together, machine and method form a reliable pair, ideal for accumulating hours and transforming experimentation into everyday practice.

That leaves aerodynamics, where the biplane pays a price: each wing disturbs the other, creating interference and drag. Engineers responded with an offset between planes, an optimized spacing-to-chord ratio, moderate dihedral and controlled torsion. Leading edges are stiffened, wing joints are carefully designed and masts are shaped. Some try the triplane to gain surface area without increasing wingspan, but the complexity often outweighs the benefit. The biplane remains the king of modest speeds, where maneuverability and low-speed handling are paramount. Airframes can accept more powerful engines, but drag limits the point. Gradually, monoplane cantilevers made of stiffer materials offer a faster future. However, as long as access to short terrain and ease of maintenance dominate, the biplane retains its relevance and practical charm, a sure companion for progress without burning out.

Little by little, a legacy began to emerge. Voisin, Farman, Curtiss, Sopwith, de Havilland and Breguet became technical landmarks as much as aircraft names. We learn the rigors of centering, the importance of simple reference speeds and the art of rigging to keep the airframe straight and sound. Tuning notebooks, time trials and workshop inspections establish a professional culture. Decades later, training biplanes like the de Havilland DH.82 Tiger Moth continue to train pilots thanks to their honesty in flight and affordable maintenance. Far from being a detour, this era of robust biplanes gave us a method: observe, measure, correct, repeat. It also imparted a taste for efficient simplicity, where every mast and cable has a purpose. Thus, from the fragile aeroplane was born a reliable tool, which paved the way for faster monoplanes without losing the wisdom patiently acquired by taming the air.

2.5 - The first records and air shows

No sooner had the first aeroplanes left the ground than a simple yet powerful idea was born: compare, measure, break records. To make these feats credible, rules were established. The Aéro-Club de France, then the Fédération Aéronautique Internationale founded in Paris in 1905, set clear categories: distance, duration, speed, altitude. Stewards controlled departures and arrivals, approved stopwatches validated times, and sealed barographs recorded altitude. In the field, pylons mark out the circuits, forcing drivers to make clean turns. This framework transformed the isolated exploit into a technical sport. Newspapers publish rankings and diagrams, manufacturers offer prizes, and flying schools feed on precise feedback. At every meeting, centering, settings, winds and fuel are discussed. The sky becomes an open runway where we learn together. Thanks to measurement and arbitration, aviation is acquiring a common language that accelerates progress and secures challenges.

Before the great encounters, a few records were set along the way. Wilbur Wright's public flights at Le Mans in 1908 established the idea of controlled, reproducible flying. In France, Henri Farman flew a kilometer in a closed circuit under official supervision, proving that a plane could take off, turn, return and land without cheating the wind.

This verified "round trip" changes everything, as it eliminates the need for a favorable wind and imposes precision. Engineers, stopwatches in hand, test wing profiles, incidence angles and control surface settings. Pilots learn to maintain approach speed and negotiate turns without losing altitude. The obsession with a clean trajectory and measurable turn radius replaces the simple straight line. Each timed flight provides numbers that can be compared from field to field. Little by little, the method became established: same aircraft, same circuit, same control, and fine-tuning until the next record.

The popular spark was ignited by the Grande Semaine d'Aviation de la Champagne, near Reims, in the summer of 1909. For eight days, a huge marked-out circuit welcomed aeroplanes of various styles, lined hangars and an amazed crowd. The rules were public, the prizes numerous and the officials scrupulous. Pilots like Glenn Curtiss, Henri Farman and Louis Paulhan distinguish themselves here, demonstrating three ways to shine: go fast, go far, go higher. The mechanics stretched the tarpaulins at dawn, the runway directors placed the pylons, the stewards sealed the barographs. Spectators follow average speeds, cumulative distances and validated altitudes on display boards. The press illustrated the trajectories, explained the notion of average speed and popularized the word "tour". This meeting proves that an aircraft can link regular loops, plan its refuelling and respect the rules. Aviation was no longer a surprise; it was now a recognizable discipline.

Amid all this hustle and bustle, one cup fanned the flames of friendly rivalry between nations: the Gordon Bennett Aviation Cup, dedicated to speed. Each country selects its champions, the rules standardize the course and the measure becomes implacable. To win, you need a smooth engine, a precisely designed propeller and a clean airframe to reduce drag. Teams work as if in a race shop: carburetion adjusted for humidity, wing angles checked against the gauge, tires controlled, weights tracked. Pilots practice keeping a constant speed, negotiating turns without stalling, managing the initial climb to avoid wasting fuel. This attention to detail benefits everyone. Parts improve, testing methods become more professional, and engineers learn to link every tenth of a second gained to a concrete modification. The Cup created a common grammar of performance that would be used for both racing and utility flights.

Soon, meetings were multiplying and traveling. Brescia in Italy attracted celebrities and curious technicians; Doncaster and Blackpool in England tested the organization on grassy fields; in Los Angeles, a large gathering on the Dominguez plain introduced aviation to the American public. Each airfield becomes a school: we learn how to orient ourselves using ground markers, how to read the wind from the smoke, and how to manage a crowded runway. Demonstrations include short take-offs, tight turns, precise landings, and sometimes mail-carrying trials to show how useful they can be. Around them, a small economy takes shape: fuel suppliers, repair shops, propeller manufacturers. Posters and programs explain event categories, pilot profiles and records to be broken. This world tour set the standards for hospitality, safety and maintenance that would later help the airfields to become true aerodromes.

In just a few years, the record-breaking curve took off. Average speeds far exceeded those of the first flights, distances exceeded hundreds of kilometers, and altitudes climbed to unexpected heights. Symbolic crossings, such as those of inland seas, proved the growing reliability of engines and airframes. Airshow meetings impose essential reflexes: weather briefings, aircraft weighing, control checks, departure and arrival procedures. Pilots learn to manage fatigue, fuel, engine temperature and wind drift as they would a workshop dashboard. Engineers, for their part, capitalize on the data and design finer machines. Thanks to this alliance of show, rule and measurement, aviation is moving from isolated feats to collective progress. Records, far from being mere trophies, became milestones pointing the way to safer, more useful and more ambitious flights.

Chapter 3: Major Aircraft Types

3.1 - Gliders, ultralights and motorgliders

Gliders, microlights and motorgliders all share the same secret: efficiency. The glider carries no engine in normal flight; it transforms altitude into distance thanks to a long wingspan and a thin wing. Performance is measured by glide ratio: with a glide ratio of 30, a glider can cover 30 kilometers, losing 1 kilometer of altitude in calm air. The best gliders exceed 50, a sign of meticulous design and lightweight materials. To stay aloft, the pilot "reads" the sky: well-formed cumulus clouds, spiraling bird silhouettes, dust sucked up by a bubble of warm air. Each clue reveals a lift to turn to gain meters. This way of flying teaches patience and anticipation: choosing a clean trajectory, saving speed, sometimes accepting to leave an average zone to reach a better one. Flying without a motor means understanding the atmosphere from the inside, and feeling that the sky becomes a partner rather than an obstacle.

Why does a wing carry air? Its shape deflects air downwards and creates an upward force. The angle of attack is the inclination of the wing in relation to the relative wind; too low and it doesn't carry much, too high and it stalls. On a modern glider, ailerons control roll, elevator pitch and vertical stabilizer yaw. Airbrakes extend from the top of the wing to increase drag and aid landing. Some gliders carry water ballast to help them cross descending areas at higher speeds, then jettison it before approach. Well-centered weight and a low-drag wing make all the difference on a course. Learning these gestures means learning the grammar of the sky: listening to the variometer, keeping the needle coordinated, taking care with the glide. Little by little, technique becomes instinct, and you discover that a good adjustment is worth as much as a great stroke of luck. This understanding, patiently acquired, makes the glider a demanding but fair teacher.

An ultralight, or motorized ultralight, is all about simplicity. It's a small, motorized aircraft designed to fly slowly, take off quickly and consume little fuel. There are classic control models with a cabin, and pendular models where a flexible wing is suspended from a cart. The principle remains the same: a light airframe, a reliable engine, moderate speeds and clear procedures. The equipment is minimal but relevant: anemometer, altimeter, radio, sometimes GPS; the key is precise piloting and knowledge of the local weather. Flying low and not too fast, you can see the landscape, find your bearings on the ground, and learn to respect trajectories and spacing. ULM offers a practical school of aeronautical common sense: pre-flight checks, weight and balance, energy management on approach. This philosophy shows that a simple, well-maintained and well-piloted aircraft can offer a safe and joyful flight.

The motorglider bridges the gap between the two worlds. It's a glider with an engine that can be used to take off on its own, or reignited en route if the lift disappears. On some models, the propeller retracts into the nose or emerges on a pylon, to then regain its purity of form in gliding flight. Two uses coexist: the "self-launch", which takes off without a tug, and the "sustainer", which is used as a back-up to return to the field. The pilot climbs with the engine until he encounters lift, then cuts off and makes a series of silent transitions, ready to restart if the air mass weakens. This flexibility extends safety and range, while preserving the art of gliding. The same fine-tuning, the same quest for finesse, with an added bonus: autonomy when the weather wavers. The motor glider learns to manage two energies, fuel and altitude, to better enjoy both pleasures.

Flying with little power requires a method. With a glider, you spot thermals under small cumulus clouds, dynamic lift along a slope, or a wave behind a mountain. You draw a mental circuit with clearance areas, calculate the safety height before each branch, and adjust your speed to the air mass. The variometer tells you whether you're going up or down, but it's the eye that chooses the best line. In microlight flying, we favour simple weather, maintain stable approach speeds and manage crosswinds with coordinated actions. Up-to-date maps, minimum altitudes, sufficient fuel: rigor makes freedom possible. These habits, learned early on, remain valid on all aircraft. They transform the pilot into a calm decision-maker, capable of transforming a capricious breeze into a clear and pleasant trajectory. The exercises repeated locally refine the pilot's touch and reinforce his vigilance.

This family of aircraft has another merit: it brings aviation closer to nature. The glider glides along in silence, showing the geography of air masses; the microlight flies gently over landforms, inviting us to respect our neighbors. Clubs, instructors and workshops all share the same culture of transmission, made up of briefings, flight logs and repeated gestures. Many pilots start out here, gaining precision, discipline and confidence, then moving on to other licenses if they wish. You'll discover that a good take-off starts on the ground, that a good landing begins well in advance of the runway, and that a simple aircraft well flown is worth more than a sophisticated aircraft badly used. In this school of efficiency, every meter of altitude counts and every choice has a meaning. To understand these machines is to understand aviation as a whole, and to give yourself wings for wider adventures, step by step. You'll learn to share the skies with other users, in harmony.

3.2 - Single- and multi-engine propeller aircraft

A propeller-driven aircraft converts the engine's energy into thrust by turning one or more blades, like a wing turning in circles. Single-engine versions use a single, simple and economical engine, ideal for training, leisure travel and local missions. Multi-engine models use two or more engines, for greater power, cruising speed and carrying capacity, with invaluable redundancy in the event of damage. In both cases, the recipe is similar: a light airframe, a well-designed wing, a reliable engine and a suitable propeller. Pilots learn to play with three interrelated variables: rpm, propeller pitch and power output. Harmonious tuning reduces fuel consumption and noise, while preserving mechanical parts. These aircraft fly at moderate speeds, take off in relatively short strips and accept a wide range of operations. Their strength lies in their versatility, perfect for discovering aviation and progressing without missing a step.

Propellers are powered by two main engine families. The piston engine, often four-stroke with magneto ignition, burns an air-fuel mixture in cylinders and transforms piston thrust into crankshaft rotation. The engine's appeal lies in its simplicity, low maintenance costs and fuel economy at low altitudes. The turboprop, on the other hand, is a small gas turbine that drives a reduction gearbox connected to the propeller. Compressed air is heated by combustion, the flow turns the turbine, then the propeller provides most of the propulsion. This system offers an excellent power-to-weight ratio and good performance at altitude, with superior cruising speeds. Both technologies use adapted controls: richness to dose fuel to the pistons, timing and torque to adjust a turboprop. What they have in common is regularity: temperature, oil pressure, rpm and vibrations are monitored like sheet music, because a happy engine makes for an efficient propeller and a comfortable flight.

A propeller blade is a turning wing: its profile deflects air backwards and creates forward thrust. The key parameter is called pitch, the angle at which the blade bites the air. With a low pitch, you get good acceleration on take-off, but you'll "grind" at cruising speed; with a high pitch, cruising speed improves, at the cost of a longer take-off distance. Fixed-pitch propellers offer a simple, lightweight compromise. Variable-pitch, or constant-speed, propellers use a governor that adjusts the pitch to maintain a target rpm: the pilot sets the rpm, and the mechanics take care of the rest. Other functions exist: feathering to align the blades with the wind and reduce drag in the event of a failure, or inverted pitch on turboprop aircraft to brake on landing. Properly adjusted, a propeller transforms every horsepower into useful meters, smoothly and efficiently.

On a single-engine aircraft, the art lies in managing energy with finesse. Before flight, we check weight and balance, airframe condition, fuel and oil, then test magnetos and, if present, carburetor heat. On take-off, we choose a climb speed adapted to the obstacle or the best rate, then settle into cruise at stabilized power. At altitude, the mixture is depleted to keep temperatures moderate and save fuel. On approach, anticipate: stable trajectory, progressive configuration, speed held until the threshold. On short or soft ground, we use a precise technique, with careful rotation and a clean flare. The limits are clear: a single engine means less available power , increased weather caution and calculated distances. On the other hand, the aircraft is forgiving, less expensive and trains excellent reflexes. Properly piloted, a single-engine aircraft flies far, calmly, turning every liter into useful kilometers.

Multi-engines add power and, above all, redundancy. If one engine is lost, the other can still propel the aircraft, provided that asymmetry is controlled. When one propeller pushes on one side and not on the other, the aircraft tends to veer off course; the pilot counters with the rudder pedal and keeps a slight inclination to the right side to stay aligned. Speed is essential: below a certain threshold, the rudder is no longer effective enough; above a reference "blue line", the aircraft climbs even on a single engine. Identify the engine at fault, check it, reduce drag by feathering the propeller if possible, and fly clean, symmetrical and precise. This discipline requires training, but brings real benefits: better performance, increased safety margin in cruising conditions and additional options in mountainous or hot terrain. It also teaches rigorous parameter setting and strict adherence to speed limits.

These aircraft families cover an immense range of uses. Single-engine piston planes train pilots, connect villages, photograph, measure and map. Fast twin-engine aircraft transport urgent freight, technical crews or provide scheduled regional services. Modern turboprops, with multi-blade composite propellers and digital controls, combine economy and regularity on short runways. Avionics have followed suit: precise GPS, reliable autopilot, clear screens and trajectory alerts. On the airframe side, composite materials reduce weight and resist fatigue well; anti-icing systems and "scimitar" propellers improve safety and efficiency. But the principle remains the same: a clean wing, a well-tuned propeller and a methodical pilot make all the difference. Choosing the right aircraft, respecting speeds and careful preparation make the sky accessible. As you learn the art of propeller handling, you'll discover a close, fine and intelligent form of aviation that makes you want to go that little bit further.

3.3 - Jets and supersonic aircraft

A jet plane moves forward by rapidly expelling a stream of heated air backwards. The engine swallows the air, compresses it with a compressor, ignites it with fuel, then the turbine recovers energy to turn the compressor again. Finally, the nozzle accelerates the gases like a backward-facing hose: the reaction pushes the aircraft forward. Unlike the propeller, which "screws" the air, the thrust of a turbojet remains effective at high speed and altitude. Mach numbers are used to compare speed with the speed of sound: Mach 0.8 corresponds to around 80% of the speed of sound. As speed increases, aerodynamics change: shock waves appear, drag increases and skin temperature rises. To resist, you need solid materials, slender wings and well-designed air intakes. Jet flight was born of a simple idea, but it required precise design at every stage.

Pioneers made the theory visible. In Germany, Hans von Ohain flew the Heinkel He 178 in 1939, the first jet to take off under its own power. In the UK, Frank Whittle had been pushing the same idea for years; the Gloster E.28/39 took to the skies in 1941, proving the reliability of a British turbojet. The first jet fighters soon appeared: the Messerschmitt Me 262 and, opposite it, the Gloster Meteor, both operational in 1944. Their advantages were clear: high speed, rapid climb, less vibration than a piston engine. Their challenges are just as clear: high fuel consumption, materials under stress and the need for wings adapted to transonic regimes. These machines force engineers to learn fast: cooling hot parts, refining compressors, filtering turbulence that disrupts air intake. In just a few years, the jet went from a discreet prototype to a production aircraft, capable of real, measured missions.

After the war, the jet transformed civil transport. The de Havilland Comet ushered in the era of commercial jets in the early 1950s, with a pressurized cabin, high flight and shorter range. The French Caravelle popularized rear-mounted engines, reducing cabin noise and improving wing aerodynamics. The Boeing 707 sets the standard for high-speed long-haul cruising, soon followed by many other models. To save money, the turbofan engine was adopted: a large fan sends a volume of "cold" air around the hot core, giving plenty of thrust with less fuel and noise. Wings were fitted with supercritical airfoils, power-assisted and then electric controls, and cockpits were modernized. The result: steadier, higher, faster flights, and commercial aviation that links continents and cities with a reliability measured in millions of hours.

Reaching the speed of sound required another step. At around Mach 1, the air compresses, shock waves form and the center of lift shifts, making the aircraft unstable if the wing is not adapted. Engineers responded with swept wings, very thin airfoils and the "area rule", which smoothes the fuselage to reduce transonic drag. On October 14, 1947, the Bell X-1, a winged rocket piloted by Chuck Yeager, exceeded Mach 1 in controlled flight, paving the way for X-planes and systematic research into high-speed stability. Later, supersonic fighters adopted shock-controlled air intakes, refined fuselages and powerful flight controls. The nozzle is sometimes fitted with an afterburner: fuel is reinjected after the turbine for extra thrust, very useful for short take-offs or acceleration, at the cost of high fuel consumption. Supersonic means precision, clear margins and disciplined piloting.

The dream has spread to commercial airlines with some exceptional aircraft. Concorde, cruising close to Mach 2 at an altitude of 18 kilometers, uses a thin delta wing, ramped air intakes and a structure capable of withstanding the heat. The Tupolev Tu-144 explores a similar path, with its own technical solutions. These aircraft prove that it is possible to link large cities in record time, but their use remains limited: sonic boom, high fuel consumption, authorized routes mainly over oceans, and high maintenance requirements. Yet they leave a valuable legacy: mastery of high-temperature materials, fine shockwave capture, and expertise in low-incidence delta wings. They also taught us that good speed is not enough; you need an economic model, appropriate logistics and compatible traffic rules. This lesson continues to inspire engineers in their quest for fast, responsible aircraft.

Today, most airliners use highly efficient turbofans with high bypass ratios, while fighter jets combine powerful turbojet engines, afterburning and aggressive aerodynamics to handle supersonic flight smoothly. Air inlets prevent lift-off, wings and fuselages work together to limit drag, and fly-by-wire controls help the pilot stay within the safe envelope of flight. Composite materials lighten, numerical calculations optimize every curve, and sensors monitor temperatures, vibrations and margins. Whether it's flying at Mach 0.85 at cruise speed, or breaking Mach 1 for an intercept, a jet remains a conversation between energy, shape and temperature. To understand this conversation is to see how an idea of reaction becomes a fluid journey. And it's also an invitation: to learn, to test, to respect limits, to go fast, far and, above all, well.

3.4 - Helicopters, gyrocopters and tiltrotors

Three families of aircraft prove that you can fly without a long runway by taming the air with blades. The helicopter uses a large motorized rotor to create lift and thrust, enabling it to take off vertically, hover over a point or move backwards. The autogyro, designed by Juan de la Cierva, lets its rotor turn freely in autorotation thanks to the relative wind, while a propeller drives it forward. The tiltrotor combines the two ideas by tilting its motorized nacelles from vertical to horizontal position, like a plane that takes off like a helicopter and then crosses like a turbine. These three solutions share a common principle, the rotating wing, but each favors a different compromise between maneuverability, speed and fuel consumption. Behind these very different silhouettes lie very concrete mechanical, aerodynamic and piloting choices. To understand their controls, their limits and their strengths, is to discover a different kind of sky grammar, based on precision and a keen ear for the wind.

The helicopter transforms rotation into lift, thanks to a main rotor whose inclination and pitch can be varied. Two key controls operate the blades. The collective changes the pitch of all the blades at once to rise or fall, as if increasing the "bite" of the air. The cyclic tilts the rotor plane to move forwards, backwards or sideways. Pedals control the tail rotor, often a tail rotor, to prevent the airframe from turning under the effect of engine torque. A swashplate transmits these commands to the rotating blades, an impressive mechanical feat. As the aircraft accelerates, it benefits from a cleaner lift, known as the translational effect. Variations exist, such as the streamlined fenestron or the NOTAR system, which uses a jet of air to counteract the torque. Since Igor Sikorsky and his VS-300, this architecture has been used for mountain rescue, winching, surveillance and precise landings where no runways exist.

A famous feature of helicopter piloting is autorotation. If power is lost, the pilot lowers the collective to reduce pitch, maintains speed and lets the air rise through the rotor. The flow then drives the blades like a mill, storing kinetic energy. On the landing flare, he briefly raises the collective to transform this energy into lift and land short. This exercise, repeated in training, shows that the helicopter is not condemned to permanent power, provided that speed and altitude are managed methodically. Flying with rotating blades also means having to deal with the asymmetry of lift between the advancing and retreating blades. Engineers respond to this with flapping joints, adapted profiles and speed limits. These technical details explain why a helicopter prefers to fly moderately fast, where its rotor remains efficient and stable, while retaining the extraordinary freedom of slow translation and hovering.

A gyrocopter chooses a different route. Its rotor is not continuously driven by the in-flight engine, but rotates freely in autorotation because the airflow created by forward motion turns it. Lift comes from the rotor, but traction comes from a propeller, at the front or rear, which pushes the aircraft. This architecture does not allow hovering, but it does offer great stability, very low stall speeds and ultra-short touchdowns. On departure, a small pre-launcher can accelerate the rotor to reduce take-off distance. When cruising, the gyrocopter likes moderate winds, which it crosses smoothly thanks to a lightly loaded rotor disk. La Cierva developed this idea in the 1920s to solve the problem of loss of control in slow aircraft, and the formula has inspired simple, robust, modern leisure aircraft. Flying a gyrocopter is all about controlling speed and attitude, while keeping the rotor disk well supplied with relative air.

The tiltrotor combines the vertical access of a helicopter with the cruising efficiency of an airplane. On take-off, the nacelles and their large rotating propellers point upwards, providing vertical thrust that lifts the aircraft. In transition, the nacelles gradually tilt forward. The wing then takes over for lift, while the rotors become horizontal thrusters. This maneuver requires sophisticated controls to maintain balance when two worlds intersect: that of the rotor and that of the fixed wing. Transmissions link the engines so that only one can drive both propellers in the event of a failure in certain phases, a vital safety detail. Once level, the aircraft flies fast and far, closer to a conventional turboprop in terms of fuel consumption and speed. Programs such as the V-22 and AW609 illustrate this ambitious compromise, useful when you need to leave a roof, fly long distances and then land in a small area.

Rotary wings come in ingenious configurations to meet specific needs. The tandem with two main rotors, as on a large transport, distributes loads without a tail rotor and excels at lifting. The coaxial configuration superimposes two counter-rotating rotors on the same axis, which cancels out torque and compacts the machine, making it ideal for confined spaces. The geared rotors, emblematic of Kaman, cross each other without touching thanks to fine synchronization, gaining in lateral efficiency. Whatever the layout, the key is to ensure that energy is well managed. The pilot anticipates the wind, keeps altitude margins, knows his speeds and monitors temperatures and vibrations. Maintenance follows, attentive to blades, gearboxes and joints. These habits turn skill into lasting safety. Behind the glass cabins and the whistling disks, a lesson emerges for every curious young aviator: with method and respect for limits, the air becomes a faithful ally.

3.5 - Modern balloons and airships

Lighter-than-air aircraft are based on a brilliantly simple idea: if you replace the air inside an envelope with a lighter gas, or with heated air, the whole thing floats thanks to Archimedes' buoyancy. Balloons use this principle without a motor, while airships add propulsion and rudders for steering. In a hot-air balloon, a burner raises the temperature of the air, lowering its density. In a gas balloon, non-flammable helium provides lift; in the past, hydrogen was used. To ascend, heat is added or a little ballast is jettisoned; to descend, the envelope is allowed to cool or gas is evacuated. It's all about balancing mass and volume, with constant attention to wind and weather. These devices don't seek record speed, but gentle stability and endurance, ideal for understanding how the atmosphere carries, pushes and sometimes surprises.

The modern hot-air balloon consists of an envelope of tough fabric, often ripstop nylon, a basket of wicker or composite materials, and a propane-fuelled burner. Before takeoff, the envelope is first inflated with cold air using a fan, then heated so that it straightens. The pilot operates two simple controls: the burner handle to add heat, and the valve at the top, called the parachute, to evacuate hot air and lose a little lift. The horizontal trajectory depends on the wind; you choose the altitude that offers the desired direction, as the air layers can blow differently. Safety relies on clear briefings, stable weather, avoidance of power lines and a clear landing site. On the ground, a team follows the flight in a vehicle to retrieve the gondola. This quiet discipline shows that piloting is above all about anticipating, reading the sky and dosing energy to transform heat into a gentle climb and then a careful landing.

The gas balloon has no burner: the envelope contains helium, which is lighter than air, and the crew carries sandbags as ballast. To ascend, a small amount of ballast is jettisoned; to descend, a valve is opened to let a small quantity of gas escape. This fine pipe makes for very enduring flights in calm weather. A special version, the sounding balloon, is launched worldwide by weather services: a large latex balloon carries a radiosonde that measures pressure, temperature, humidity and wind. As it inflates, the balloon rises to the stratosphere, then bursts when the latex reaches its limit, generally between twenty and thirty kilometers above sea level. The probe descends with a small parachute. These vertical profiles, repeated daily, are used for climate forecasting and research. They are a reminder that static flight is not just a poetic adventure, but also a precise scientific tool, capable of mapping an invisible sky.

An airship is a lighter-than-air craft with propulsion and controls. A distinction is made between non-rigid blimps, where the shape comes from the slight internal overpressure, and semi-rigid blimps, which have a keel supporting the payload. Air-filled balloons, driven by fans, maintain the shape and adjust the centering. Pylon-mounted motors drive propellers, some of which are steerable, while rudders and elevators stabilize the trajectory. Navigation remains cautious: best results in light to moderate winds, typical speeds close to 80 to 120 kilometers per hour, but remarkable endurance. Helium ensures safety, and soft acoustics enable long missions over cities or coastlines. This combination of economy and precision explains its use in observation, cartography, scientific research and advertising, where visibility and stability are more important than pure speed. On the ground, the aircraft attaches to a mooring mast, facilitating upwind orientation and boarding operations.

Operating a balloon or an airship requires special logistics. The choice of weather window is crucial: storms, shears and strong gusts are avoided. Crews prepare the weight and center of gravity, plan alternate landing sites and coordinate ground recovery. For an airship, an airstrip team manages the mast, mooring lines and wind rotation; for a balloon, the team quickly recovers the envelope and gondola after landing. Modern materials, such as coated fabrics and composite structures, make the whole lighter and more UV-resistant. Avionics simplify navigation, with GPS, transponders and reliable radios to share airspace safely. Helium, which is safer than hydrogen, remains precious, and is saved by careful management of leaks and pressure. This patient organization shows that success depends on preparation: good briefings, repeated gestures and constant respect for wind limits.

Modern balloons and airships teach a lesson in elegance: flying doesn't necessarily require great noise or enormous power, but a careful balance between mass, volume and weather. The hot-air balloon reveals the dance of the air's layers and teaches patience; the gas balloon shows the finesse of adjustments; the airship proves that you can move slowly but surely with remarkable autonomy. These machines are used to observe fragile environments, measure the atmosphere, film, train pilots and share a peaceful sky with other users. They remind us that a successful flight begins on the ground, with lucid choices, simple checks and an inquisitive eye for the wind. By understanding how air carries a giant envelope as easily as a boat floats on water, we discover another gateway to aviation: that of quiet efficiency, which transforms a steady breath into a controlled journey.

Chapter 4: The Forces That Make You Fly

4.1 - Lift, drag, weight and thrust

Four forces govern every moment of flight: lift that lifts, drag that brakes, weight that pulls down and thrust that propels. Imagine a hand sticking out of a moving car. If you tilt it, the air deflects it and a force pushes it up or down. A wing does the same thing, but much better. In stabilized flight, lift balances weight and thrust compensates for drag. If one changes, everything else must adjust. Increasing speed boosts lift, but also increases some drag. Reducing incidence reduces drag, at the risk of losing support. The pilot manages this puzzle with his stick, rudder pedals, power and sometimes devices such as flaps or airbrakes. To understand these forces is to understand why we take off longer in warm air, why a stable approach is prepared far in advance of the runway, and why a well-coordinated turn keeps lift effective rather than wasting it in slips.

Lift arises when the wing deflects air downwards and receives an upward force in return. Its intensity depends above all on the wing's surface area, speed and angle of attack, i.e. its inclination to the relative wind. Too weak, and the wing carries little; too strong, and the flow lifts off, leading to a stall, a phenomenon in which lift suddenly drops. Engineers design airfoils to delay stall, sometimes adding slats or flaps. These devices increase camber and effective surface area, useful for low-speed lift during take-off and landing. Birds teach the same idea when they spread their feathers before landing. For the pilot, the key is to adapt incidence to the situation: more speed in turbulent air, less in calm air, and a constant eye on trim and coordination so that the wing works in a clean, predictable flow.

Drag is the force that opposes movement. It combines parasitic drag, due to the shape, roughness and friction of the air, and induced drag, linked to the lift itself. At low speeds, the wing has to produce a lot of lift, and induced drag dominates; at high speeds, friction and shapes take over. Between the two, there's a zone of minimum drag, which is of great economic interest. Fairings, smooth surfaces and well-sealed joints reduce parasitic drag, while a longer wingspan attenuates induced drag by reducing wingtip vortices. Extending landing gear or flaps increases drag, which sometimes helps to descend without accelerating. The pilot learns to keep the aircraft clean when he wants to go far, and to "brake with the wing" when he wants to lose altitude without exceeding his speed, a delicate art that protects the flight envelope.

Weight is the vertical force due to gravity. It depends on total mass, including fuel, and acts at the center of gravity. The position of this center changes according to load distribution. Too far forward, the aircraft becomes stick-heavy and needs high speed on approach; too far aft, it becomes nervous in pitch and may stall. The manuals define a safe C of G range, checked before the flight with a weight and balance. In a turn, the lift must not only compensate for the weight, but also provide the centripetal force. The wing therefore works harder and the load increases, which is measured in load factors, expressed in "g". The tighter the turn, the higher the g, and the higher the stall speed. Knowing these effects avoids surprises close to the ground, and helps you choose the right speed for a short turn while retaining a margin of lift.

Thrust comes from the engine and propeller. The propeller acts like a spinning wing, accelerating the air backwards to create a forward reaction. Its efficiency varies with rpm and blade angle, hence the interest in variable-pitch propellers that maintain optimum rpm. The turbojet engine compresses, heats and ejects air, delivering powerful thrust at high speed and altitude. Turbofans mix a large "cold" flow with a hot core to increase efficiency and reduce noise. At low speeds and on short runways, the propeller's responsiveness shines through; in fast cruise, reaction dominates. Altitude, temperature and wind influence thrust and take-off distance. The pilot anticipates this by calculating his weight, choosing his configuration and respecting torque, rpm and temperature limits, because well-managed propulsion transforms energy into useful meters with regularity.

When thrust equals drag and lift equals weight, speed and altitude remain stable. To climb, the aircraft needs excess thrust or power; to accelerate, it must temporarily overcome greater drag. Without an engine, a glider advances by consuming its altitude, and chooses a best glide speed to cover the greatest distance. On approach, we play with two reservoirs of energy, altitude and speed, to arrive on the runway with just the right amount of both. Flaps allow you to carry at reduced speed, at the cost of greater drag, useful for short descent and precise landing. The weather changes the picture: hot air or high altitude reduce performance, while a headwind helps with take-off and landing. Knowing how to read these forces and their interplay transforms an average flight into a clean, calm and safe one, where every choice has a clear physical reason.

4.2 - Wing profile, camber and angle of attack

The airfoil is the "slice" you'd see if you cut a wing like a chopstick. This shape guides air around the wing and deflects it slightly downwards, creating an upward force. The leading edge is the rounded front edge, the trailing edge the thin rear edge, and the chord the line connecting these two edges. Thickness and curvature influence the way the air flows: a profile that's too steep disturbs the flow, while a well-designed profile makes it smooth and efficient. On the upper surface, air speed increases and pressure drops; on the lower surface, pressure remains slightly higher. This imbalance, combined with downward deflection, provides lift. A wing is not just a plane: it's a sculpture of air designed to carry without wasting energy. We then fine-tune this geometry by testing various nose radii and relative thicknesses.

Camber describes the average curvature of the profile. Imagine a line down the middle of the wing, from front to back: the more it arches, the greater the camber. Positive camber helps generate lift even at low angles of attack, which is useful for short take-offs and slow flight. Conversely, low or almost zero camber is ideal for high speeds, when you want to reduce drag. Thickness also plays a role: more volume can house a solid spar and fuel, but too much thickness increases resistance. The leading edge must remain sufficiently rounded to tolerate a wide range of incidences; the trailing edge, which is thin, neatly closes the flow. A highly cambered profile facilitates short landings but limits maximum speed; a flatter profile accepts fast cruising. Engineers compare these compromises on curves that link lift, drag and moment. The result can be summed up simply: camber regulates low-speed ease, thickness takes the strain, and together they decide the character of the wing.

47

The angle of attack is the angle between the wing chord and the relative wind, i.e. the direction in which the air hits the wing. By pitching up, we increase this angle: lift increases, but so does drag. As long as the airflow stays together, the wing works well; beyond a critical angle, the air stalls and lift drops. This limit depends on the wing's profile, camber, surface finish, flaps and load. The same aircraft can therefore take off and land more slowly with flaps, as they allow lift at lower incidence. The pilot doesn't read the angle directly: he manages attitude, indicated airspeed and feel in the controls to stay in the effective zone. Gusts and tight turns require margins, as the load increases and the stall speed climbs. Properly managed, the angle of attack becomes an invaluable ally in transforming speed into lift without waste.

High-lift devices modify the in-flight profile to gain lift at low speeds. Flaps are lowered, increasing camber and sometimes surface area; leading edge slats allow a trickle of air towards the upper surface to delay lift-off. The result is a "kinder" wing close to the ground: shorter take-offs, slower approaches and comfortable round-offs, at the price of increased drag that has to be managed. Surface quality counts as much as design: a clean wing keeps a thin layer of air glued on, while dirt, insects or ice roughen the flow. This layer, known as the boundary layer, can remain laminar over a few zones, then become turbulent; the important thing is that it doesn't stall too soon. The pilot chooses the configuration according to runway, wind and weight, then adjusts the attitude to stay well clear of the critical angle. Used properly, the wing "changes shape" on demand, offering real safety margins.

The planform, as seen from above, completes the story. High aspect ratio, i.e. long span and short chord, reduces induced drag: ideal for gliders seeking endurance. A stockier wing is better able to withstand high speeds and maneuvers, useful for fast aircraft. At the tips, winglets limit wingtip vortices, improve cruising efficiency and sometimes stabilize roll. Designers also add torsion, known as washout: the tip carries slightly less than the root, which delays wingtip stall and keeps the ailerons efficient. Finally, we adjust the angle of incidence, a fixed angle between the wing and the fuselage, so that the aircraft flies at a comfortable cruising attitude. In this way, profile, camber, incidence, aspect ratio and tips work together: the wing is not a single choice, but a coherent whole designed for the mission in hand. A trainer favors tolerance, while a record-breaker aims for finesse.

For the pilot, these ideas become concrete choices. On take-off, we use the recommended configuration to gain lift at low speed, then maintain an attitude that keeps a margin on the critical angle. At cruising speed, we look for the attitude and power where the profile works cleanly, without pitching up unnecessarily or letting drag climb. On approach, a stable speed, adapted to the weight and flaps, keeps the wing in a safe zone even if a gust occurs. As you turn, the load increases and so does the stall speed: coordinate with the rudder so that the wing doesn't waste its lift in a slide. In cold weather, you need to keep an eye on the icing, which adds weight and roughens the surface; in hot weather, take-off distance increases. Learning to read profile, camber and angle of attack is like taming the air itself, and this lucidity turns every flight into a clear and motivating lesson.

4.3 - Ailerons, elevator and steering

On an aircraft, three axes govern each movement: roll, pitch and yaw. Three control surfaces respond to these axes: ailerons roll, elevator pitches up or down, rudder turns the nose left or right. The pilot controls these surfaces with two main gestures. The stick, pushed or pulled, adjusts pitch via elevator; tilted left or right, it activates the ailerons. The rudder pedals, two pedals on the floor, move the rudder. A clean turn requires coordination of these actions: a little aileron to bank, enough elevator to maintain lift, and just the right amount of rudder to keep the nose on track . Without coordination, the plane slides or skids, which increases drag and can be surprising. The learning process consists in feeling the balance, with the help of outside eyes and instruments. We aim for a centered log, a stable attitude and a decided inclination, so as to transform gestures into clean, reproducible trajectories.

Ailerons are small surfaces articulated to the trailing edge, placed near the wingtips. When one moves up and the other down, lift decreases on one side, increases on the other, and the aircraft rolls. This movement is not neutral: the descending aileron increases drag and tends to pull the aircraft to the opposite side, a phenomenon known as reverse yaw. To counteract this, we add a little rudder on the turning side. Designers help the pilot with differential ailerons, which rise more than they descend, and with Frise ailerons, whose protruding leading edge creates compensating drag when the aileron rises. The wing can also carry a slight dihedral, which naturally stabilizes the bank. In practice, you engage the roll with the stick, follow with the rudder, then gently recenter the ailerons to hold the chosen angle. The desired result is a smooth, yaw-free turn, with the aircraft well coordinated and the ball calmly centered.

The elevator lives at the tip of the horizontal tail. By turning it downwards, it pushes the tail upwards and causes the aircraft to pitch; upwards, it pitches the aircraft up. This play modifies the angle of attack of the wings and therefore the lift. Pulling is not just climbing: at a given speed, it increases the g-load, which can bring the aircraft closer to a stall. So we prefer to fly with energy: choose a speed, set the power, then maintain attitude with small movements. Trim relieves the effort by adjusting a small area or the incidence of the stabilizer. Some models use a one-piece stabilizer, which is very effective. Centering is very important: too far back, and the elevator becomes too sensitive; too far forward, and you have to pull hard. On approach, you maintain your target speed by first adjusting your trim, and then using power to hold the slope. A well-managed elevator produces calm, predictable trajectories.

The rudder, linked to the vertical fin, controls yaw. It aligns the nose with the airflow, compensates for engine torque on take-off and keeps the turn clean. When taxiing and at the start of the run, we press down firmly with the right foot to stay on the axis, as the propeller can rotate the aircraft due to asymmetry of the airfoil and blade. In the air, you keep an eye on the ball: centered, flight is coordinated; off-center, the plane slips or skids. Steering is also used to cope with crosswinds. On short final, you'll often land in a crab, then straighten up with the rudder and bank slightly to windward to keep the axis. You can also practice gliding on approach: aileron bank, opposite rudder, increased drag to lose altitude without accelerating. At high speeds, we avoid sudden kicks that load the structure; on fast aircraft, a yaw damper helps to calm oscillations.

Behind these gestures, precise mechanics transmit orders. Cables, pulleys, rods and linkages transform a centimetre of control stick into degrees of rudder. Balancing weights in front of the shaft reduce effort and limit vibration. Some control surfaces are fitted with tabs to assist or compensate; a small servo-tab can turn a large control surface with less effort. Heavier aircraft use hydraulic boosters, followed by electric fly-by-wire controls, where computers interpret the pilot's commands and protect the flight envelope. The objective remains the same: precise, predictable response. Before each flight, we check for free travel, direction of movement and the absence of hard points. In flight, we listen for clues: a too-firm control stick is often a sign of excessive speed or an unsuitable configuration; a slack control stick alerts us to the proximity of a stall. A healthy control chain makes the finesse of piloting visible.

Training exercises provide lasting reflexes. In level flight, you practice standard-rate turns, keeping altitude and ball centered; in climb and descent, you maintain your chosen speed without letting it drift. In slow flight, hold the axis with the rudder and support the wing with the control column, then recognize the early signs of a stall. On take-off, anticipate rudder correction; in turbulence, loosen your grip a little and let the plane live without over-piloting. On multi-engine aircraft, the failure of one side reminds you of the importance of a firm footing and a clean attitude. Little by little, we no longer "operate" parts: we orchestrate forces. Ailerons set the inclination, depth sets the energy, steering polishes the trajectory. This music becomes natural when each gesture has a clear reason. Mastering these three control surfaces means giving the sky a calm, sure response, and opening the door to more ambitious flights.

4.4 - Stability, balance and load factors

Stability describes how an aircraft reacts after a small disturbance. If it returns to its initial state on its own, it is stable; if it deviates, it is unstable; if it remains in the new position, it is neutral. A distinction is made between static stability, the immediate tendency after disturbance, and dynamic stability, the way in which oscillations are subsequently damped. Three axes count: longitudinal for pitch, lateral for roll and directional for yaw. Designers look for a compromise: enough stability to reassure and dampen, but not too much to maintain maneuverability. A trainer will be very docile, while an aerobatic aircraft will accept lower stability, controlled by precise piloting. On a day-to-day basis, we observe the attitude, speed and log: if, after a small impulse, the aircraft calmly refocuses itself without effort, stability is doing its job. Understanding these reactions transforms anxiety into a clear reading of forces and guides simple gestures.

Longitudinal stability depends above all on the position of the center of gravity (CG) in relation to the aerodynamic center of the wing. Placed slightly forward, the CG creates a natural tendency to return to a neutral attitude, as the horizontal tail provides a restoring moment, often by pushing down slightly. This margin is called the static margin: too little, and the aircraft becomes nervous; too much, and it becomes stick-heavy. The horizontal stabilizer and elevator regulate this torque. Trim balances the effort to hold a speed without pulling or pushing. Flaps modify camber and shift forces: when extended, the nose can rise or fall according to geometry, necessitating a slight readjustment on the control column. Power also has an influence: propeller blast, thrust line and torque effects can pitch up or down. A well-designed aircraft remains predictable: small variations in speed or attitude are responded to by a gentle return to equilibrium, which the pilot then fine-tunes with the trim.

Lateral and directional stability depend on the shape, seen from above and from the front. A slight dihedral, i.e. wings that rise towards the tips, helps the aircraft to straighten out in roll: as it tilts, the low wing receives more angle and regains more lift. The vertical stabilizer provides course stability, like a weathervane that likes to line up in the relative wind. A swept-back wing and high fuselage add a keel effect that further stabilizes. But roll and yaw talk to each other: an aileron strike can create reverse yaw, and a heading disturbance can trigger a roll, giving oscillations known as Dutch roll. Designers use a combination of dihedral, vertical stabilizer and shock absorbers to avoid these oscillations. On the other hand, an aircraft may have a tendency to tilt insensitively and turn wider and wider, a phenomenon known as spiral divergence, which the pilot corrects with vigilant wing control and proper coordination.

Centering transforms theory into concrete action. Before the flight, the total weight and the position of the center of gravity are checked using the leverage arms and moments indicated in the flight manual. The results must remain within the CG envelope defined by the manufacturer. If the CG is too far forward, the aircraft will be stable but heavy to pitch up, with longer rotation and flare distances; if it is too far aft, the control column will be lighter, but the aircraft will be closer to a pitch stall, and may come as a surprise. Fuel consumption, a passenger changing places or a piece of luggage being moved all affect the CG during the flight. To stay calm, load weights close to the recommended plane, secure objects and anticipate the effects of flaps and power. Keeping the target speed on approach, adjusting trim and allowing for runway margin give you flexibility. A good C of G makes for honest stability and precise control, which simplifies everything else.

The load factor measures how much the aircraft "weighs" in flight, compared to its weight on the ground. In level flight, it's 1g. In a steep turn, the wing has to provide more lift to compensate for the centripetal force, and the load factor rises. The higher the load factor, the greater the stall speed, according to the root of the load factor: a steep turn can therefore stall at a speed that would seem safe in a straight line. Every aircraft has structural limits, indicated by category: in general, normal category around +3.8 g to -1.52 g, utility around +4.4 g to -1.76 g, aerobatics around +6 g to -3 g. Speeds are also respected: the manoeuvring speed, known as Va, authorizes full use of the control surfaces without exceeding the planned loads, and serves as a reference in turbulence. Flying at Va in turbulent air, coordinating turns and avoiding abrupt movements protects the airframe and keeps a comfortable margin.

In the cockpit, stability, centering and load factors become habits. You take off with a well-tuned aircraft, compensate to hold your chosen speed, and keep the ball centered so that the wing works cleanly. When climbing, we respect published speeds; when cruising, we adjust the trim to take the strain off the hand; when descending, we avoid pulling too hard so as not to push the g up. Pilots learn to sense a healthy aircraft: disturbed, it returns gently; solicited, it responds without surprises. Larger aircraft often add aids such as yaw damping or electric controls to ensure that the envelope is respected, but the logic remains the same. Correctly placed weight, a flight plan adapted to the wind and coordinated movements transform energy into simple, safe trajectories. Understanding these balances doesn't just help you pass your exams: it frees your attention to look outside, make the right decisions and enjoy the sky with confidence and precision.

4.5 - Take-off and landing performance

Performance is the distance and time it takes to take off, climb and land within the safe envelope of flight. For take-off, we distinguish between ground run, rotation and total distance to clear a typical 15-meter obstacle. On landing, we talk about stabilized approach, touchdown and stopping distance to a standstill, again with or without an obstacle. It's all about energy: you need enough speed for the wing to carry, enough runway to accelerate and, on the return, enough runway to dissipate the speed without exceeding braking limits. Flight manuals give reference figures, obtained during tests and then corrected by the pilot according to weight, wind, temperature and runway conditions. It helps a lot to remember the main idea: gain lift early and brake effectively later, but only with clean movements and planned margins.

Several factors influence distances. Weight is king: heavier aircraft require higher take-off speeds and longer runs; on landing, the energy to be dissipated also increases. Air density changes with altitude, temperature and pressure: warm air and high altitude mean "light" air, so less lift and longer distances. A headwind shortens take-off and landing by reducing ground speed; even a modest tailwind lengthens them considerably. The slope of the runway helps if it's downhill on takeoff, and complicates if it's uphill; the surface condition also counts, whether it's high grass, gravel or a wet runway that lengthens the stop. Flaps modify camber: a notch can help carry early, but too many flaps increase drag and can penalize climbing. Reading these factors means translating weather and terrain into meters gained or lost.

On take-off, three speeds guide the action. Vr is the rotation speed at which the nose is lifted off; Vx gives the best climb gradient for passing a nearby obstacle; Vy provides the best climb speed in time. On a short runway, we brake the wheels, put on full power, check the parameters, then release the brakes, accelerate straight ahead and turn at Vr. If an obstacle is waiting, hold Vx until you're over it, then accelerate to Vy for better cooling and climbing. On a soft runway, keep the nose light to reduce roll, and build up speed in ground effect before climbing. Twin-engines and jets add decision speeds such as V1, linked to the acceleration-stop distance; the idea remains the same: to know when to continue and when to stop. Careful preparation, runway markings and a clear plan turn theory into a clean, reproducible take-off.

On landing, the key is the stabilized approach: axis maintained, configuration set, power adjusted and target speed, called Vref on airliners, adapted to weight and wind. We aim for an end point, control the slope with power and speed with attitude, then round off to touch down in the target area. Flaps increase lift at low speed and drag to descend without accelerating. After touchdown, gently raise the stick to load the wheels, brake gradually and, depending on the aircraft, deploy spoilers, thrust reversers or reverse propeller pitch to shorten the stop. Wet or contaminated runways mean reduced grip and longer distances; anti-skid helps, but is no substitute for anticipation. A crosswind can be managed by crabbing and then using rudder just before touchdown, or by gliding with a slight inclination to the wind. Landing early, straight and smoothly is better than "too long too fast".

Preparing your performance means making the flight manual speak for itself. The tables give basic distances, often for a dry runway, at sea level and without wind; corrections are then applied for weight, temperature, density altitude, wind, slope and surface condition. Manufacturers sometimes supply multiplying factors for grass or wet conditions; many operators add an operating margin to retain flexibility if an actual factor differs from the forecast. A simple example helps: if the temperature rises and the wind drops, we recalculate, choose a longer runway or an adapted flap notch, and lighten if necessary. Climb performance also needs to be verified, especially with obstacles or relief: a climb rate promised on paper must become a real gradient along the trajectory. The right reflex is to convert numbers into concrete decisions before riding.

Safety comes from clear choices. Before take-off, we set ourselves a mental stopping point: beyond this point, if an essential parameter is missing, we stop. We calmly brief you on trajectory, speeds and backup configuration. On arrival, maintain a stabilized approach; if not, execute a clean go-around instead of forcing a touchdown. A short runway calls for discipline: strict speed holding, measured flare, continuous braking without blocking. Bigger machines add electronic aids and protections, but the spirit never changes: respect speeds, apply the published configuration, watch the remaining length. With practice, you read a track like a mechanic reads a plan: winds, slopes, landmarks, escape routes. Performance is no longer an abstract number; it becomes a reliable method of transforming available space into a margin of safety. This method makes the sky simpler, and every flight more serene.

Chapter 5: Navigation and Instruments

5.1 - Altimeter, variometer and artificial horizon

In the cockpit, a trio of instruments form the pilot's inner compass: the altimeter, the variometer and the artificial horizon. Together, they tell you where you are vertically, how fast you're going up or down, and how the plane is tilted in relation to the Earth. When visibility drops or you're flying through clouds, this trio becomes indispensable, as our sensations can be misleading. The altimeter links the aircraft to the pressure of the atmosphere and converts this pressure into altitude. The variometer translates small changes in pressure into climb or descent rates. The artificial horizon creates a reliable horizon, even at night, to maintain the correct attitude. Taken separately, each tells part of the story; together, they form a complete sentence that guides decisions. Learning to read them means learning to trust numbers rather than impressions, to keep a clean, steady and safe trajectory, from take-off to landing.

The altimeter resembles a large watch, but its pointer reads the static pressure sensed on the fuselage. Inside, aneroid capsules contract or expand according to air pressure; a mechanism transforms this movement into altitude. Because the pressure changes with the weather, the instrument is set with the setting knob. QNH displays the altitude relative to sea level, and must coincide, on the ground, with the elevation of the airfield. QFE displays height above terrain, useful for reading circuit height directly. Above the transition altitude, we switch to the standard setting of 1013 hPa (29.92 inHg), so that everyone speaks the same language. Beware of cold temperatures: the real atmosphere may be "tighter" than the model, so the altimeter overestimates the height. So we learn to check: needle "lives" on takeoff, matches elevation, and cross-references with radio or GPS. Properly set, the altimeter becomes a graduated vertical ruler.

The vertical speed indicator, the variometer, tells the music of the flight: ascents and descents. It compares the current static pressure with that of a few seconds ago, thanks to a calibrated orifice; from this difference is born a needle that indicates hundreds or thousands of feet per minute. This instrument has a slight delay, which is normal, and which we learn to anticipate by looking first at the attitude and then at the variometer. In light aircraft, it is used to maintain a stable rate of climb on approach, or to check a climb predicted by the artificial horizon. In gliding, we use "total energy" electronic variometers which correct the effects of acceleration and sing in audio: a rapid beep signals a climb, a low tone a descent. A good reflex is to smooth your movements: maintain speed, correct gently, and confirm the trend over a few seconds rather than "chasing the needle". The variometer guides, but it's the attitude that commands.

The artificial horizon, or attitude indicator, produces a stable horizon using a gyroscope that keeps its plane in space. It features a stylized sky and ground, and a small aircraft silhouette to indicate pitch and roll. Historically driven by a vacuum pump or electric motor, the instrument can drift a little and must remain within its tilt limits. Modern AHRS systems use digital gyroscopes, accelerometers and magnetometers to estimate attitude, with greater resistance to prolonged acceleration. Whatever the technology, the idea is the same: to provide a reference that is independent of our sensations, which can be wrong in prolonged turns or at night. Before departure, we check our erection: the horizon must be horizontal on the ground. In flight, we hold a target attitude (for example, five degrees nose-up on a climb) and cross-check it with the variometer and altimeter to validate the trajectory. If the instrument seems to be frozen, we suspect a malfunction and reduce our confidence.

These three instruments interact to produce their own gestures. On take-off, the altimeter "comes alive", the variometer displays a positive rate, and the artificial horizon confirms the climb attitude: the coherence of all three signals a healthy trajectory. In cruise, a tiny stick adjustment seen on the artificial horizon should announce, a few seconds later, a slope on the variometer, then a slow evolution on the altimeter: cause, effect, result. On approach, we set an attitude corresponding to the target speed, adjust the slope with power and monitor the variometer to stay within a comfortable range. In poor visibility, the method becomes more rigorous: maintain attitude, check vertical trend, confirm assigned altitude. In a turn, we keep the pitch attitude, control the ball and make sure the altimeter doesn't inadvertently drop. This calm choreography transforms numbers into clear trajectories, and gives the pilot a steady gaze, even when the real horizon disappears.

Like all machines, these instruments have limits that the pilot learns to recognize. A clogged static plug freezes the altimeter and misleads the variometer; a reverse leak can cause fanciful indications. A vacuum pump failure can cause a mechanical horizon to fall off; cross-checking with the heading indicator, perceived attitude and the outside becomes vital. In winter, frost on the orifices alters the reading; in summer, heat changes the density and reminds us to anticipate margins. The answer is always comparison: if the attitude shows a level-off, but the variometer plunges sharply, we check power, configuration and attitude; if the outside contradicts the horizon displayed, we suspect the instrument is dubious. Modern airplanes add a number of backups: a folding horizon, a second static source and redundant sensors. Before each flight, simple checks are carried out: altimeter set to QNH indicating elevation, variometer at zero, horizon well erected. This hygiene turns three dials into reliable allies.

5.2 - Indicated speed, true speed and Mach number

Pilots talk about three speeds that are similar, but don't serve the same purpose: indicated airspeed (IAS), true airspeed (TAS) and Mach number. Indicated airspeed is what the on-board instrument displays, thanks to the pitot-static system; it tells us how hard the air is pushing against the aircraft, and therefore how hard the wing is working. True airspeed, on the other hand, measures the airplane's speed through the air mass, useful for navigation and travel times. Mach number compares the plane's speed to the speed of sound, a key point when flying high and fast. Three numbers for three needs: wing safety (IAS), planning and economy (TAS), control of compressibility effects (Mach). The units help to make sense of it all: IAS and TAS are expressed in knots or kilometers per hour; Mach has no unit, it's a ratio. Knowing what is what avoids confusion and turns a dashboard into a clear source of information.

The indicated speed comes from a duo: a Pitot tube measures the total pressure in the relative wind, and a static plug measures the ambient pressure. The difference between the two, translated by the instrument, gives the IAS. As the wing reacts to pressure, all limiting speeds (stall, flaps, gear, turbulence) are published in IAS. Minor instrument and position errors are then corrected to obtain the calibrated speed, CAS. At low speeds and altitudes, IAS and CAS are very close. As speed and altitude increase, the air becomes slightly more compressed and the indication becomes too optimistic; this is known as the compressibility error. Engineers then introduce the equivalent airspeed, EAS, which removes these effects. In practice, what pilots remember most is this: fly the safety speeds in IAS, because that's what the wing smells like; check for proper trim and the absence of plugs on the intakes; compare with other sources if the reading seems odd. A clean kite is a well-informed kite.

True airspeed indicates how many nautical miles or kilometers the aircraft travels through the air mass. With altitude, the air becomes less dense. To obtain the same lift, the wing keeps the same IAS, but as there are fewer molecules, the plane actually moves faster: the TAS increases. Practical rule of thumb: the TAS increases by around 2% per thousand feet if the temperature is standard. Thus, an IAS of 120 knots at around 10,000 feet gives a TAS of almost 144 knots. Temperature also counts: warmer air increases the TAS for a given IAS, colder air decreases it. On-board computers calculate the TAS from altitude, temperature and pressure; failing that, a calculation rule or application provides a good estimate. TAS is used to plan flight times, estimate fuel consumption and check that the aircraft is achieving its expected cruise performance.

There's another speed that pilots often consult: ground speed. It comes from the GPS and measures displacement relative to the ground. Ground speed is the TAS corrected for wind. A headwind reduces it, a tailwind increases it; a crosswind imposes a drift angle. To keep a clear course, you point your nose into the wind, which creates a triangle of speeds: heading, course and wind. You can draw it on a chart or let the computer solve it. Example: TAS 140 knots and headwind 20 knots give 120 knots ground speed, so a longer trip. Conversely, 20 knots astern gives 160 knots of ground speed and a time saving. Understanding these relationships avoids surprises and explains why a "slow" flight can go fast, or why a fast aircraft takes longer in a strong wind.

Mach number compares aircraft speed with the speed of sound in air. At 15°C near sea level, the speed of sound is around 1,225 km/h;

the colder the air, the lower this speed. At altitude, fast aircraft therefore use Mach as a reference, for example Mach 0.78 or 0.82 in cruise. When the local flow reaches the critical Mach on the wing, shock waves form, drag rises and the center of lift shifts: this is the transonic regime. To stay safe, we respect a limit known as the MMO, or maximum operating Mach. Airfoils and inlets are designed to delay these effects, and pilots monitor a machmeter. Interesting contrast: IAS can drop on climb as Mach increases, because the speed of sound decreases with temperature. The automatic systems then switch from maintaining IAS to maintaining Mach. This reference avoids entering an uncomfortable and inefficient shockwave zone.

In the cockpit, these speeds work together like teammates. On take-off and landing, we fly at published IAS speeds, as the wing reacts to pressure. On climb, we hold an IAS of best slope or best rate; yet the TAS climbs naturally with altitude. On fast aircraft, we switch from holding IAS to holding Mach as the temperature drops and cruise approaches. In navigation, we plan with TAS, check actual advance with ground speed, and adjust heading to compensate for wind. The classic pitfalls are easily avoided: don't confuse TAS and ground speed, set the altimeter and keep the holds clean, respect the speed limits in IAS. With these points of reference, a dashboard becomes legible, and each number tells its own story. You can then pilot with method, and every trip becomes a clear exercise in managing energy and time with precision and confidence.

5.3 - Compass, VOR, ILS and GPS

Navigating means knowing where you are, where you're going and how to get there safely. The magnetic compass is the simplest reference: a graduated card floats in a dampened bath and aligns itself with the Earth's magnetic field. The compass reads a magnetic heading, which has to be corrected for local variation, the difference between magnetic and true north, and sometimes for the aircraft's own deviation due to metal masses and electrical currents. Before departure, the compass is compared with the heading indicator and the map, the variation indicated is noted, and the instruments are adjusted. In straight flight, the compass is reliable; in turns or under acceleration, it delays and, worse, lies a little. So we learn to use it when the aircraft is stable, to confirm with other sources, and to keep an open map. This habit transforms a modest little instrument into a solid anchor for keeping a clear course.

The compass likes stability, but the pilot often moves. When turning, it is subject to particular errors. On an easterly or westerly course, acceleration makes it appear to turn north, while deceleration makes it appear to turn south; on a northerly or southerly course, it delays or precipitates the indication as you enter the turn. To work properly, use a gyroscopic heading indicator or HSI. Before taxiing, it is aligned with the compass at the fixed point; in flight, it is readjusted from time to time, as gyros drift slowly. Turns are made at the standard rate of about three degrees per second, controlled by the turn indicator or HSI index, which makes it easier to intercept the course. The simple rule remains valid: heading and log. Keep the ball centered on the rudder, hold the trim on the stick, and periodically check that compass, tiller and chart are telling the same story. Three eyes are better than one.

The VOR, for VHF Omnidirectional Range, is a ground-based radio beacon that transmits radials numbered 001 to 360. The aircraft, equipped with a receiver, selects a course with the OBS button; the CDI needle indicates whether you are to the left or right of this radial, and a TO/FROM flag specifies the direction. You identify the station by listening to its Morse code, guaranteeing that you're using the right frequency. To join a radial, intercept at a reasonable angle, then recenter the needle by small adjustments, ball centered. The VOR operates in radio visibility: the higher you are, the greater the range. Two stations allow you to cross radials and fix a position. A classic error is reverse sensing, when the needle is read backwards; this can be avoided by checking TO/FROM and intended heading. Used properly, the VOR transforms the map into invisible rails, useful in variable weather and for maintaining a measured heading.

The ILS, Instrument Landing System, guides an aircraft on a precision approach. The localizer, a VHF transmitter aligned with the runway, provides the lateral axis; the CDI's horizontal needle shows whether to correct left or right. The glide slope comes from the glide, a UHF signal directed towards the approach, displayed by a vertical needle which instructs to climb or descend to stay within about three degrees. The procedure is standard: intercept the localizer first, stabilize, then capture the slope from below to avoid a false indication. We check the Morse identifier, set the published heading and follow the minima: decision height below which we don't descend without seeing the runway. Aids sometimes replace the markers with a DME. Even with autopilot, vigilance remains the same: attitude maintained, power adjusted, target speed respected. The ILS is not a magnet; it's a fine line to be followed calmly, keeping the needles refocused.

GPS, part of a family called GNSS, uses satellites to send the exact time and position. The receiver measures the time it takes for the signal to arrive; with at least four satellites, it calculates latitude, longitude, altitude and time, then displays heading, ground speed and course. To navigate, you link points called waypoints; the Direct-To page leads to one of them, while a route links several segments. The screen indicates the lateral deviation, which is reduced by gently correcting the heading. Augmentation systems, such as WAAS or EGNOS, improve accuracy and enable highly precise non-precision approaches. But GPS doesn't explain the wind, it doesn't replace fuel reading and it can lose signal; it's crossed with map, compass and VOR. Used properly, it simplifies situational awareness and reduces the calculation load, freeing the mind for anticipation and flight management. A glance outside remains the best confirmation.

Each tool has its own personality; the art lies in getting them to work together. In visual navigation, you set a course and time on the chart, then keep your heading with the preserver and compass, while the GPS confirms ground speed and drift. En route, a VOR verifies position, and course is adjusted to match trajectory. On approach in poor visibility, an ILS provides axis and slope; the GPS acts as a situational awareness assistant, the map remains open, and the checklist unfolds the steps. The key words are identification, stabilization and anticipation. Identify the beacon, stabilize the attitude, anticipate corrections. Three checks are better than one brilliant improvisation. This calm method transforms a cockpit into a reliable team: instruments, procedure and outside view complement each other, so that a trip becomes a series of small, clear and reproducible decisions. This is the heart of serene piloting.

5.4 - Aeronautical charts and flight planning

An aeronautical chart is the pilot's toolbox for understanding space, terrain and rules before taking off. A distinction is made between VFR charts, designed for visual flight, and IFR charts for instrument flight. The difference lies in the level of detail and radio information. The scale indicates precision: the smaller the denominator, the finer the view of obstacles, villages and landmarks. The legend explains colors, aerodrome symbols, frequencies and airspace boundaries. Elevation lines and hypsometric tints show the relief; square figures, the highest elevation in the quadrant, indicate the highest obstacle in an area. Approach charts, vertical profiles and aerodrome diagrams complete the picture. Understanding this graphic grammar enables you to transform a complex region into a legible route, marked out with safe altitudes, turning points and frequencies ready for use in your logbook.

Reading a map means first of all identifying who controls the sky. Airspace classes, marked by specific contours and colors, indicate the altitudes applicable and the associated service. CTRs and TMAs define controlled aerodromes; RMZs or TMZs require radio or transponder. R, P or D sectors, respectively restricted, prohibited or dangerous, require activation verification before departure. Obstacle symbols, wind turbines and power lines help you choose a comfortable altitude. The relief in successive shades reminds us that a valley wind can surprise an aircraft that's too low. ATIS, tower, approach and flight information frequencies appear near the fields. Pictograms indicate parachuting, aerobatics, gliders, helisurfaces or hydrosurfaces. Cross-referencing these clues builds a mental image: where I can go, who I can call, what minimum height I can keep, and what pitfalls I can avoid. A well-read map makes navigation simpler than the horizon might seem.

Flight preparation starts with the weather and NOTAMs, messages announcing construction work, unavailable beacons, closed runways or active zones. METARs and TAFs describe the present and probable evolution of wind, visibility and clouds; upper wind charts help you choose course and level. Pressure and temperature are checked to anticipate density altitude, especially on short runways. On the performance side, weight and balance must remain within the manual envelope, not forgetting the impact of baggage and fuel. The fuel rule includes a contingency reserve and a credible clearance. We note the expected QNH, the presence of waves, potential icing or thunderstorms, and set conservative personal limits. NOTAMs also specify the actual activation of R or D zones and the status of radio aids. This stage transforms numbers into concrete decisions: leave earlier, choose another runway, add a notch of flap, or carry less weight.

Plotting a VFR route involves linking obvious landmarks at regular intervals: confluences, interchanges, lakes, ridges, identified antennas. We select an altitude that clears the relief and respects the spaces, then calculate the magnetic heading, taking into account variation and wind. A ruler-rapporteur and an E6B or an application give ground speed, drift and time between points. A navigation log is prepared with headings, times, fuel, frequencies and minimum altitudes. An alternate airfield is chosen, with its map and circuits. In flight, you compare map and terrain, confirming with GPS without stopping to look outside, and noting the time crossed at each point. If a cloud gets in the way, we apply the diversion procedure: safety heading, radio call, simple recalculation, then clear announcement. This calm, ground-based approach transforms navigation into a series of small, easy-to-follow steps.

In IFR, engineering changes scale. En-route charts show airways, VOR radials, DME distances and minimum sector or route altitudes. SIDs guide the exit, STARs lead to the approach, and approach charts describe axes, altitudes, slopes and minima. A structured briefing summarizes frequencies, intercept headings, platform altitude, OCA/H minima and turn-around procedure. Nearby obstacles and the minimum safe altitude around the initial fix are highlighted. The choice of IFR diversion is based on published minima and forecast weather at the time of arrival, with fuel for holding and go-around. RNPs require verified GNSS integrity; an ILS requires verification of Morse identifiers for localizer and glide. Here again, the map is not decorative: it tells a precise story. Following it step by step transforms a cloud into a marked corridor, where every number has a purpose.

EFB tablets and applications make it easy: up-to-date maps, integrated weather, vertical profiles, automatic calculations and track recording. Yet one golden rule remains: redundancy. Keep a paper source or a second device, charged batteries and a backup plan if the electronics go out. Opening and closing a flight plan, announcing intentions, keeping checklists and briefing passengers and crew all contribute to safety. Simple methods help you decide: PAVE to evaluate pilot, aircraft, environment, mission; 5P to regularly reassess the situation. After the flight, a short debrief connects the map to the experience: course too ambitious, point wrongly chosen, frequency forgotten, perfect margin elsewhere. Each correction makes the next preparation more fluid. Reading, plotting, briefing, checking, then adjusting in flight: this routine transforms a sheet covered in symbols into a reliable companion, and each route into a clear lesson that makes you want to explore a little further.

5.5 - Essential aviation meteorology

Weather shapes every flight, because air is never empty or still. It has a pressure, temperature and humidity that change its properties. When the air is warm, or when the aerodrome is at altitude, it becomes less dense: lift decreases, the take-off run lengthens and the climb weakens. This is summarized by density-altitude, which increases with heat and altitude. Conversely, cold, dry air improves performance. Ground pressure, expressed in hectopascals, is used to set the altimeter so that the altitude reading is accurate. Humidity also has an influence: humid air warms and cools differently, sometimes favoring fog or low clouds. For a pilot, therefore, the weather is not a decoration but an invisible driving force: it determines the length of runway required, the speed to be maintained and reasonable margins. Learning to read these quantities is akin to reading the personality of the sky, in order to transform a changing environment into stable, predictable trajectories.

Wind arises from pressure differences: air flows from high-pressure zones to low-pressure zones, while being deflected by the Earth's rotation. Close to the ground, friction slows and bends the flow; at higher altitudes, it becomes more aligned with the isobars. Gusts are brief accelerations, while shear is a sudden change in force or direction with altitude. To take off straight, we prefer a headwind; when taxiing and running, rudder pedals and stick keep the axis. In the air, we compensate for drift by pointing the nose slightly into the wind to keep us on course. Sea breezes, valley breezes and relief effects can create local winds that differ greatly from regional forecasts. A windsock tells you a lot: it indicates direction, approximate intensity and the presence of gusts. Reading the wind means choosing a suitable runway, altitude and speed, then keeping a flexible attitude to its whims.

Clouds are useful signatures. In an unstable atmosphere, humid air rises, cools and condenses into cumulus, sometimes cumulus congestus, then cumulonimbus if energy is abundant: showers, turbulence and lightning are born. A stable atmosphere spreads moisture into stratus or nimbostratus, giving low ceilings, drizzle and reduced visibility, but little shaking. In between, altocumulus and altostratus often herald the approach of a warm front. High-lying cirrus clouds signal the arrival of moisture and wind aloft. Fog is the result of very humid air coming into contact with cold ground or night-time cooling: it requires patience and a clear field. Near mountains, motionless lenticular clouds betray a powerful wave and possible rotors downwind. For the pilot, recognizing these patterns helps to anticipate air quality, the likelihood of rain, ceiling evolution and a reasonable departure time. Observing, comparing and then linking clouds and in-flight sensations transforms weather into a readable ally, rather than a surprise.

Fronts mark the boundary between air masses. A cold front pushes in warm air, which rises abruptly: we expect showers, squalls, gusts and a rapid drop in temperature, then an improvement after the passage. A warm front slides over the cold air, piling up cloud layers: cirrus, altostratus, then stratus with continuous rain and low ceilings. When they mix, occlusion combines these effects. Pressure drops before a front, rises afterwards, and wind often jumps from one sector to another as it passes. Thunderstorm lines, , which align active convective cells, call for respect and a wide turnaround. In preparation, we identify the position, speed and trajectory of fronts on maps, then adapt departure, route and altitude to avoid the worst zones. Understanding these mechanisms is not remote theory: it decides on a safe slot, a realistic clearance and a fuel reserve compatible with detours.

Turbulence has many faces. Mechanical turbulence is caused by the wind rubbing against terrain, forests or buildings, especially when the air is cold and the wind is strong. Convective turbulence arises from air bubbles heated by the sun and rising during the day. At higher altitudes, shear zones sometimes create turbulence in clear air, invisible to radar. Near mountains, the flow forms waves and sometimes rotors downwind: powerful but predictable if you read the signs. Frost appears when supercooled droplets hit the aircraft in near-zero air: it makes the aircraft heavier, increases drag and degrades lift; it can be avoided by changing altitude, leaving a cloud or using approved systems. Cumulonimbus clouds combine all the risks: severe turbulence, hail, downbursts and lightning. The rule of thumb is simple and effective: fly well around them, respect distances, and prefer a detour to a risky crossing.

To decide, pilots combine observations and forecasts. METARs describe the present weather; TAFs forecast its evolution. Maps show winds and temperatures aloft, fronts and thunderstorm zones; radar and satellite images locate rain and convection; SIGMETs signal dangerous phenomena. Pilot reports, PIREPs, add the experience of those already in the air. At the briefing, realistic personal limits are set: minimum ceiling, visibility, acceptable crosswinds, icing levels to be avoided. En route, you re-evaluate with weather reports and your own observation, compare options and don't hesitate to postpone, divert or wait if margins shrink. Keeping a simple log of conditions encountered, linking observed sky and aircraft behavior, then debriefing on the ground transforms experience into solid reflexes. The weather then becomes a patient conversation with the atmosphere, and each flight a lesson that enlarges confidence without ever narrowing caution.

Chapter 6: Flying rules and safety

6.1 - Licenses, ages and training paths

The world of pilot licenses resembles a ladder with well-defined rungs. Each rung combines theoretical knowledge, practical skills and a responsible attitude. You don't just learn to "hold" a stick; you learn to decide, communicate and respect common rules. Licenses are divided into categories: glider, balloon, ULM, airplane, helicopter, drone. Depending on your dream mission, you choose the appropriate course, from soaring to traveling between airfields. The principle remains constant: progress through measurable objectives, validated by an instructor and an authority. Each course combines theory, dual control and supervised solo flights. Cross-cutting skills are added: radio phraseology, meteorology, performance and human factors. As mastery grows, so do privileges: flying farther, carrying passengers, crossing certain spaces. The result is not just a piece of paper, but a verifiable level of confidence. This scale rewards regularity, preparation and curiosity, transforming a dream into a safe practice.

Ages and conditions vary from country to country, but there are common benchmarks. In Europe (EASA), as a rough guide, a first solo flight in an airplane is often around age 16, and can go down to age 14 in a glider; a private airplane license is obtained around age 17, while gliders and balloons are accessible around age 16. In the United States (FAA), the student pilot certificate is available from age 16 for airplanes and 14 for gliders/balloons; the private license is available from age 17, the professional license from age 18, and the air transport license from age 23 (21 under certain conditions). An appropriate medical certificate is required: class 2 for private licenses in Europe, LAPL medical for the light sector, class 1 for career pilots; on the FAA side, class 3 is often sufficient for private pilots. We also require a command of aeronautical English, a verified identity and, for minors, the agreement of their legal guardians. These benchmarks provide guidance, but the local authority publishes the precise thresholds, which are applied in conjunction with the school.

The training process generally begins at an approved flying club or school. You meet an instructor, get to know the aircraft and take an introductory flight to get a feel for attitude, coordination and the outside view. Next come the theory lessons: aerodynamics, weather, performance, navigation, regulations and human factors. A schedule alternates between ground briefings, simulator and real flights, with a precise progress log. The logbook records each lesson, the time spent in dual control and the hours flown in supervised solo. When the instructor is satisfied that the student is safe, he or she authorizes the first solo, a milestone that validates the student's budding autonomy. The next phase includes aerodrome circuits, navigation to other airfields, radio management and complete flight preparation. Before the practical exam, a theory test verifies knowledge, then a tester evaluates briefing, decision making, piloting and safety. This step-by-step progression transforms learned gestures into reflexes, and proves that a clear method opens the door to the sky.

For light aircraft, two private routes sum up the basic spirit. A leisure license authorizes simple local trips with a shorter program; the full private license is aimed at longer navigations and controlled areas. In both cases, there is a common core: dual training, supervised solo, "triangle" navigation to two external airfields, and preparation for a safe daytime flight. A night rating can be added early on to learn approach, visual illusions and appropriate phraseology. The glider and balloon courses offer a very accessible entry point for many young people: early soloing, training in reading the wind, finding lift and choosing a landing site. The number of hours is reasonable but serious; the important thing is not speed, but regularity. Weekly training stabilizes skills, while long breaks force you to revise. With this patience, the license becomes a passport: take a passenger, join a field, then dare ambitious navigation.

Beyond the basics, qualifications quickly broaden your horizons. Instrument flying teaches you to maintain heading, altitude and speed without a visible horizon, and to follow procedures, minima and go-arounds impeccably. Multi-engine flying teaches asymmetric management, feathering and speed discipline. Aerobatics reinforces precision, load factor management and knowledge of limits. Other modules are available according to region: mountain, seaplane, classic train, ICAO English, international radiotelephony, instructor. For the career, we add more advanced theories, a professional license, and then the privileges required for public transport. The professional route favors regular hours, strict medical records and an even more formal safety culture. But all benefit from the same reflexes: clear briefings, applied checklists, cautious decision-making and strict adherence to the flight envelope. These successive layers don't pile up badges; they gradually transform a leisure pilot into an accomplished aviator, capable of choosing the right option at the right time.

A few practical tips will help you pave the way to your first badge. Choosing a dynamic club, visiting hangars, chatting with instructors and watching a real-life briefing are better than a posted price. Putting together a realistic budget, looking for youth scholarships, joining a cadet program or a weather course reduces the obstacles. Putting theory lessons together in short sessions and flying often consolidates memory; a small simulator at school reinforces what you've learned between flights. Reading aeronautical English and practicing phraseology aloud make you more at ease on the radio. Keeping an impeccable logbook, noting lessons learned and preparing each outing with a mini-flight plan give clarity. Finally, adopting a pilot's ethic makes all the difference: punctuality, respect for equipment, listening to personal and meteorological limits, going around without hesitation if the approach is not stable. Step by step, these habits transform training into a solid, motivating trip.

6.2 - Rules of the air and airspace

The rules of the air form a common grammar so that different pilots, on different machines, can share the same sky without getting in each other's way. Their aim is simple: to make trajectories predictable and avoid surprises. Two flight frames often cross. In VFR, we see and avoid, while maintaining comfortable visibility conditions. Under IFR, we follow published routes, altitudes and procedures, under the supervision of air traffic control. In both cases, the radio speaks a precise language: aircraft call sign, position, intention, then word-for-word readout of clearances. The controllers give headings and levels, but the pilot remains responsible for the safety of his aircraft. This discipline doesn't make flying cold or complicated; it calms it down. Everyone knows what to say, when to say it and how to act. In this way, a living sky becomes an orderly, legible and shared space, where aeronautical courtesy is a real strength.

Around an aerodrome, the aerodrome circuit organizes arrivals and departures like a traffic circle in the air. There's the initial climb, the crossing, the downwind parallel to the runway, the base, then the final axis. Most airfields use the left-hand turn, others the right-hand turn, indicated on the map. You integrate by respecting the published altitude, announcing your positions and maintaining comfortable spacing. Aircraft on final take precedence, and if necessary, you lie back to give them the right-of-way. On the ground, safety continues: taxi on the marked taxiways, stop short of the runway at the holding line, and only engage with clear authorization. Lights on, transponder set, eyes scanning long and wide, everything contributes to preventing runway incursions. The circuit teaches an essential lesson: flying is also about sharing a simple choreography, visible and respected by all.

Simple rules designate who yields the right of way. When crossing at the same altitude, the aircraft that sees the other on its right gives way and adjusts its heading early enough to be readable. When overtaking, you pass on the appropriate side, keeping a clear separation and only crossing the trajectory when clearly ahead. When approaching an uncontrolled aerodrome, the aircraft already in the circuit or on final has priority. Lighter-than-air aircraft and gliders receive special attention, as their speeds and manoeuvring capabilities differ. Helicopters, capable of hovering, announce themselves to avoid rotor-blast on others. At night or in poor visibility, light signals help: red on the left, green on the right, white at the rear. This simple code makes it possible to identify the direction of traffic and choose the right avoidance. These rules of courtesy are concrete tools that transform a busy sky into a legible scene.

Height and altitude ensure a safe distance from terrain and people. Low overflights over inhabited areas are avoided, and there is always enough height to reach a landing area in case of mechanical problems. Out of relief, cruising levels organize traffic: on a magnetic route in one sector, you choose different altitudes from those in the opposite sector, and visual flights often add a "plus five hundred" margin to offset instrument flights. This vertical separation reduces head-on crossings. Visibility and distance from clouds complete the picture: flying visually means seeing and being seen, which means keeping a reasonable distance from cloud banks and fog. In the mountains, we respect more generous margins and choose valley axes that allow us to turn around. Imposing these heights is not rigidity: it's a safety cushion that transforms the unexpected into a simple manoeuvre.

Airspaces are divided into classes, from the most controlled to the freest. Around the main runways, a control zone protects take-offs and landings, extended higher up by superimposed volumes where control separates trajectories. Entering these areas requires a clearance and the use of a dedicated frequency. Elsewhere, some sectors simply require a radio or transponder to be seen and heard. Certain zones exist for a specific reason: temporary prohibition, military activity, special training or protection of a sensitive site. These are noted on maps and specified by information messages. The pilot prepares his route to avoid what is closed, bypass what is active and cross what is accessible with the requisite approval. This geography of the sky is not intimidating when you know how to read it: it resembles a city map, with its fast avenues, quiet streets and supervised crossroads.

The pilot's responsibility is to prepare, communicate and decide in good time. You read up-to-date charts, consult advisories and file a flight plan when required. You set your transponder correctly, keep your ear to the ground and follow clearances word for word. In the event of unforeseen circumstances, announce early, propose a simple solution and follow instructions. Personal margins remain the best insurance: if visibility drops, you lengthen or reroute; if the crosswind exceeds your comfort level, you change terrain. Keeping a clear logbook of the areas overflown, noting frequencies and minimum altitudes, briefing passengers and crew - all these things help you gain serenity. These rules are not barriers, but guard rails. They enable us to learn, to progress and to welcome other users of the skies with respect. In this way, the freedom to fly remains a safe, shared and lasting pleasure.

6.3 - Checklists, briefings and human factors

A checklist is a small sheet of paper, but it's a big idea: turning critical tasks into simple steps to be validated. In aviation, no-one "remembers everything" from memory, because distraction always exists. As early as the 1930s, after the introduction of more complex aircraft like the Boeing Model 299, crews formalized checklists to make procedures reproducible. The principle is universal: the checklist is not a school questionnaire, it's a shared safety tool. It's used before start-up, before take-off, during cruise, on approach, and at parking. At each key moment, it recalls the essentials: fuel, controls, instruments, flaps, parameters. The pilot follows a "flow", a logical visual scan of the cockpit, then checks point by point aloud. This calm routine prevents the pilot from forgetting an unimportant detail that could get in the way of what's to come. The simpler the aircraft, the shorter the checklist, but the habit remains the same: prepare, do, check.

Two ways of using a checklist coexist, and we choose them according to the context. "Read-do" means read the item and then do the action immediately, useful when you're new to the aircraft or when the workload is low. "Do-verify" means executing a complete flow by memory, then checking the items on the checklist, useful for crews and rhythmic phases. The challenge-response format, where one person asks the item and the other responds, reinforces the quality of listening. Normal checklists cover planned phases; shorter emergency checklists remind you of vital actions to be carried out without delay, such as switching off a power source or choosing a gear. Their secret is not length, but clarity: simple words, logical order, legible font. We revise them as the aircraft evolves, and test them cold on the ground. Above all, we avoid "reciting" them mechanically; we live them, by really checking what we're reading. This attention transforms a sheaf of paper into a reliable second memory.

The briefing is the spoken version of the flight plan: it aligns ideas before taking action. Before take-off, we specify the runway, wind, initial heading, reference speeds and configuration. We add a key phrase for the unexpected close to the ground, for example the point at which we stop on long runway or the safe trajectory in case of insufficient power. En route, a mini-brief recalls altitude, airspace and expected weather; on arrival, we describe circuit, axis, target speed, go-around and credible clearance. The TEM (Threats, Errors, Margins) method helps you to think calmly: what are the possible threats, what are the frequent errors, what are the expected margins. As a crew, we share tasks, check that everyone has understood his or her part, then keep a simple catchphrase if something surprises us. Briefing doesn't mean reciting poetry, it means creating a highly legible mental map, which avoids unnecessary improvisation and makes each step predictable, even when the air becomes turbulent.

Human factors remind us that the pilot is human before being a decision-making machine. Our attention is limited, our working memory forgets quickly, and our senses can be misleading, especially without a horizon. Fatigue reduces alertness and lengthens reaction times; excessive stress closes the field of vision. The solution is methodical: proper sleep, hydration, breaks, simple briefings and coherent checklists. We also keep an eye on the workload: too many actions in a short space of time leads to forgetfulness. It's better to slow down, take control and put things back in order. Sensory illusions exist, such as believing you're going uphill when you're accelerating, or feeling a bend when you're going straight ahead; the artificial horizon then becomes the judge. Mistakes are not a disgrace, they're a signal: we announce them, correct them, note them down so we can avoid them later. Keeping a small experience diary, with conditions, decisions and lessons learned, transforms hours of flying into visible, lasting progress.

Teamwork, known as CRM, transforms a crew into a reliable system. Everyone announces what he or she is doing, checks what the other says, and dares to speak up if he or she perceives a discrepancy. The words are short and standard: heading, altitude, speed, clearance reread word for word. During taxiing, take-off and approach, conversations not related to the flight are kept to a minimum, in line with the "sterile cockpit" principle, which leaves plenty of room for critical tasks. Communication with control follows the same logic: structured message, active listening, immediate correction if something seems incoherent. Cross-reading avoids pitfalls: one sets a frequency, the other confirms; one lowers the flaps, the other looks at the indicator. Anticipating the next phase and sharing intentions calms the workload. In a light aircraft, the passenger can help: hold the map, spot a runway or keep an outside eye on . CRM isn't just for big planes: it's a state of mind that makes every flight clearer and more serene.

A few simple habits link checklists, briefings and human factors. We follow the triptych "pilot, navigate, communicate" in this order: first attitude and speed, then route, then radio. We maintain clear decision points, such as a go-around if the approach is not stabilized at the planned height. We regularly check the status of the automatic systems to avoid "automatic surprises": which mode is engaged, which target is displayed, what the aircraft is going to do in the next ten seconds. The workload is kept to a minimum by early preparation of frequencies, maps and configuration. After landing, a short debrief notes what went well and what can be improved, and updates the checklist if anything is missing. This discipline doesn't take the joy out of flying, it gives it a framework. By accumulating these calm gestures, we build a robust security that frees the mind to learn, explore and progress with confidence.

6.4 - Pre-flight checks and basic maintenance

Starting a pre-flight inspection is like playing detective before becoming a pilot. The aim is twofold: to check that the aircraft is in good condition and that the planned flight is within its limits. Preparation starts in the office, with weather, NOTAMs, weight and balance, fuel, take-off and landing distances. We open the flight manual to confirm speeds and configurations, then consult the technical logbook to ensure that scheduled maintenance and inspections are up to date. This fine-tuning avoids any surprises when you get to the aircraft. Thinking "threats, errors, margins", we anticipate: strong crosswinds, short runways, heat that increases density altitude, or particular activity on the road. The pre-flight checklist then becomes a concrete roadmap. It will guide you, outside, around the aircraft in a constant direction, from the documents to the last look before take-off. The quality of this calm moment transforms the flight into a clear exercise, because you know exactly what you're leaving with.

When we arrive at the parking lot, we secure the scene before opening the canopy. A propeller is always treated as "alive": keep your hands away and make sure that your keys and battery switch are removed if you're working around the nose. We check chocks, parking brakes, control surface fasteners and pitot covers. A first general look tells us a lot: dry ground under the aircraft, no traces of oil or fuel, fairings in place, antennas intact. Inside, we confirm the presence of all obligatory documents, the condition of the checklist and maps, the freedom of the controls and the correct locking of the seats. Afterwards, we check that the batteries and circuit-breakers are in the OFF position before any external manipulation. Then we close the doors and hoods, and start the "tour" always in the same direction. This discipline ensures that no area is overlooked. Eyes, hands and nose work together: look, touch, listen and smell. An unusual smell or a suspicious noise is valuable information.

Fuel and oil deserve meticulous attention. We start by checking the actual quantity in each tank, dipstick in hand if the aircraft requires it, not just an electrical gauge. We drain the low points with a transparent test tube until we obtain a clean sample: no water at the bottom, no particles, color and odor conforming to the intended fuel. The caps are then carefully replaced: a poorly closed cap, and suction can empty a tank in flight. On the engine side, we check the oil level with the dipstick, within the range recommended in the manual; if it's too low, we top it up with the right viscosity; if it's too high, we risk venting it. Inspect hoses, visible filters and exhaust area for seepage and binding. During refuelling, connect the cargo hold and the aircraft with an antistatic strap, keep fire extinguishers accessible and stay focused. A clean, well-sealed fuel supply means the promised autonomy is actually available.

The airframe and controls tell the story of the aircraft's health. We take a look at the wing: leading edge not severely dented, canvas or sheet metal taut, rivets in place, flaps and ailerons free over the entire travel, with no abnormal play. Confirm with the stick: "left aileron, left aileron up" to check direction. If necessary, clean bugs on the leading edge with a damp microfiber: a smooth surface wears better. Pitot clear, static plugs clean, stall alarm paddle movable. On the undercarriage, check tires for pressure, symmetrical wear, brake leaks and intact shock absorbers. Under the hood, we take a look at the cables, alternator belt and air filters. At the empennage, we check the fin, elevator, hinges, counterweights and control surface freedom, then make sure the trim moves and returns. Lights, headlights, antennas and windows complete the tour. Each coherent detail is the sign of a healthy airframe, ready to translate your gestures into clean trajectories.

In the cockpit, the visit is transformed into a departure configuration. Seats locked, belts ready, items stowed so that no pen slips under a rudder. Altimeter set to QNH, horizon erected, fuel selected on the right tank, mixture and throttle at the starting point, magnetos set to OFF. After start-up, we confirm oil pressure within seconds, load indications and normal climb temperatures. At the stopping point, the engine test is not a decorative ritual: we check magnetos, carburetor or intake warm-up test, acceptable rpm drop, electric pump, alternator, variable-pitch propeller if present, instruments in the green. Controls, trimmers and flaps are rechecked for freedom and direction, according to expected performance. A final look from the outside removes chocks, covers and fasteners, checking that the area is clear. This choreography makes the takeoff clear: plane ready, pilot ready, runway confirmed, wind read. A good start always begins with a good stop.

Finally, basic maintenance protects performance over time. Many tasks are reserved for the certified mechanic and the maintenance program, but the pilot can make a useful contribution: cleaning the leading edges and propeller with suitable products, protecting the canopy from micro-scratches, maintaining tire pressures, topping up the oil, keeping the batteries charged in the hangar, fitting UV and dust covers. After each flight, note any anomalies in the logbook: unusual vibrations, fickle headlights, flashing warning lights, small leaks. It's better to stop and let others see than to "fly anyway". A regular check-up will spot incipient corrosion, loose fasteners, tired seals, clogged intake foams. Storing cards, harnesses and helmets neatly avoids silly wear and tear. This daily attention is not obsessive: it's free performance and safety. Treating the aircraft with method and respect keeps it a reliable companion, ready to teach and travel for a long time.

6.5 - Radio communications and phraseology

Radio is the common voice of the sky. It's used to see each other without seeing each other, to coordinate trajectories and to avoid surprises. An effective message follows a simple order that's easy to memorize: who I'm calling, who I am, where I am, what I'm doing or asking. Before transmitting, listen for a few seconds so as not to interrupt another pilot, then press the button and speak clearly, neither too quickly nor too slowly. Avoid unnecessary words, announce numbers clearly, and release the pedal after a short pause to avoid "clipping" the end. Radio is not a telephone: you don't chatter, you inform. Each airfield has its own frequency; some provide automatic information (ATIS) that gives wind, QNH and runway in use. Standard phraseology guides the vocabulary so that everyone understands the same thing. With these reflexes, a black box becomes a precise tool that makes air traffic flow smoothly and predictably.

On a self-informed airfield, everyone describes their actions so that they can be seen by ear. It starts with parking, then taxiing, before line-up, on final and after clearance. A typical message looks like this: "Montpellier LFxx, Fox-Tango Oscar, at club parking lot, setting off for laps, Alpha information received". Later: "Fox-Tango Oscar, at stopping point runway 30, testing completed, ready to depart for a lap". Before entering the runway: "Fox-Tango Oscar, lining up for runway 30, immediate departure". Downwind: position, altitude and intention. On final: "Fox-Tango Oscar, final 30, complete". After landing: "runway clear". You remain descriptive, keep your voice calm, and keep an eye on the outside as well: the radio helps, but the eyes remain the first line of defence. If two aircraft arrive together, you announce the lengthening or the wait to keep the runway clear and legible.

In a controlled airfield, the tower sequences movements. First, the ATIS is listened to, and the runway, wind, QNH and information letter are noted. The initial call specifies: service, callsign, position, ATIS received, request. The check authorizes starting up if necessary, then taxiing with a clear route: tracks, stopping points, runway to be joined. Critical elements are reread word for word: runway, QNH, altitudes, heading, transponder. You stop at the holding line and never enter without explicit authorization. The tower issues "ready for departure" or "cleared for takeoff", which you repeat precisely. After takeoff, the instruction may include a heading, an altitude and a frequency change; again, this is reread and executed. In case of misunderstanding, we ask "repeat" rather than "imagine". Radio courtesy means short, clean messages with a respectful tone. This rigor transforms a busy track into a safe choreography where everyone knows when to act.

En route, flight information and approaches help you cross airspace or integrate. You announce route, altitude, estimated position and intention, then request a service: radar tracking, CTR transit, climb, level change. The controller responds with a transponder code, sometimes "radar identified", reminders of points and headings or levels to hold. The elements to be collated are nonnegotiable: transponder code, altitudes, headings, space clearances. If you're crossing an arrival line, follow the published headings precisely and call back at the requested point. On arrival, you request integration: "request integration for landing", listen to the runway in use, receive a clearance and align yourself with the landmarks. The GPS helps you follow the route, but the radio sets the priorities. Keeping track of your announcements, points and readings makes your progress clear to everyone, controllers and pilots alike.

Priority for emergencies is based on key words that are understood everywhere. "Mayday" signals immediate distress; "Pan-Pan" announces a serious emergency without imminent danger. The message always follows the same pattern: callsign, nature of the problem, position and altitude, heading or route taken, intentions, people on board and fuel remaining. The controller then releases the frequency, gives priority headings or clearances, and coordinates assistance. On the transponder side, an emergency code 7700 makes the aircraft visible to all radars; a radio failure is signalled by 7600; 7500 concerns an interception and is not used by mistake. A go-around is simply called a "go-around", with the published trajectory or the one given by the tower. If you're diverting for weather reasons, announce it early, ask for a heading and inform us of the new aerodrome you're aiming for. This clarity saves precious time and turns an unforeseen event into a controlled procedure.

Good habits make phraseology natural. We note down runways, QNH, headings, altitudes and codes in a logbook; we prepare subsequent frequencies to reduce the workload; we keep a "sterile" cockpit during taxi, take-off and approach. The numbers are clearly expressed: heading two-zero-five, altitude one thousand five hundred, frequency one-two-three decimal five. The radio alphabet avoids confusion: Alpha, Bravo, Charlie, all the way to Zulu. Standard verbs simplify: "maintain", "recall", "authorized", "negative", "received". If you miss an instruction, you say so, ask for it to be repeated and read it back correctly. A well-tuned headset, a microphone close to the lips and a reasonable volume improve everything. After the flight, a short debriefing notes any messages that are unclear or too long, and suggests a clearer version for the next time. With this benevolent discipline, radio ceases to impress and becomes a discreet ally that enhances safety and confidence.

Chapter 7: Civil and Commercial Aviation

7.1 - From pioneers to mass transport

Moving from isolated exploits to travel for all required transforming the skies into a reliable network. In the early 1910s, meetings and endurance flights showed what a plane could do, but nothing was yet regular. Airmail soon proved that it was possible to keep to a schedule if the route, weather and maintenance were well planned. By 1919, commercial routes were linking major capitals, with aircraft built from sturdy airframes and adapted to carry a few passengers and mail. Crews learned to navigate by landmarks, ground lights marked out nighttime routes, and radio facilitated position reports. Each flight becomes a small chain of coordinated decisions between pilots, mechanics and ground staff. By dint of standardization, measurement and documentation, the airplane ceased to be a curiosity and became a regular means of crossing countries, then continents, with schedules announced and kept.

Airmail served as a school of rigor. Carrying sealed bags at fixed times forced improvements in maintenance, maps, forecasts and instruments. Lines were meshed and stages were organized around reliable airfields with workshops, fuel and hangars. Beacons sent radio cues, the first navigation aids made it possible to follow a route even in moderate visibility, and runway lighting made landings easy to read. Cabin comfort improved, with cleaner fairings, efficient windows and simple heaters. The arrival of mixed-haul/passenger aircraft, then of aircraft truly designed for transport, changed the economic equation. An emblematic model, the DC-3, showed that it was possible to fly fast, far and at controlled cost, opening up stable networks. Timetables, tickets, connections and the multiplication of airfields are transforming the experience: we no longer "try" a trip, we plan it and link it to other journeys.

The next step is to tame altitude. Cabin pressurization makes it possible to fly above complicated weather conditions, over long distances, with passengers breathing normally. Pioneering aircraft, followed by elegant four-engine planes, connect the oceans in short legs. On board, the role of the crews was enriched: ground operations agents, cabin crew and flight engineers ensured a fluid chain from check-in to arrival. Airlines devise adapted fares and classes of service to fill flights more efficiently. Behind the scenes, workshops apply planned maintenance programs, operations offices compare route, wind and fuel, and meteorologists refine their maps. Reliability grows when everyone speaks the same procedural language. The model proves its solidity: a well-prepared aircraft, a pressurized cabin and trained crews make long, regular and comfortable routes possible.

The jet age ushers in high-speed commercial aviation. The first civil jets led the way, soon followed by jets that became the norm on major routes: the advanced de Havilland Comet, the Caravelle, the Boeing 707 and the Douglas DC-8. Turbojet engines became more efficient, wings and air intakes more refined, and cockpits were fitted with modern aids. Airports became longer, runways were equipped with precise lighting, and control rooms used secondary radar, standardized procedures and vertical separation. Two organizations structure international cooperation: ICAO harmonizes rules and techniques between states, while IATA coordinates airlines and practical standards. En-route charts, standardized departures and arrivals, and precision approaches ensure that crews the world over speak the same grammar. The result: shorter journey times, more efficient connections, and higher levels of safety thanks to method and the comparison of experience.

The jumbo jet then paved the way for true mass transportation. The 747, DC-10 and L-1011 brought large cabins, long range and reduced costs per seat. Ground systems followed: computerized reservations, baggage containerization, telescopic gangways, hubs to concentrate and redistribute flows. Turbofans with high bypass ratios reduce noise and fuel consumption, winglets and optimized airfoils save fuel, and advanced materials lighten airframes. High-performance twins obtain permission for long ocean routes while meeting strict engine reliability requirements. Operations become a science of orchestration: fast turnarounds, planned maintenance, real-time technical monitoring, ongoing crew training. Passengers, for their part, benefit from dense schedules, varied fares, improved comfort and a worldwide network where you can change planes like you change trains, with connections thought out down to the minute.

Making mass transport safe and predictable relies on a common culture. Companies apply checklists, briefings, event reports and skills-based training. Controllers separate and guide, satellites provide advanced navigation and surveillance, and aeronautical meteorology provides accurate forecasts. Manufacturers test structures and systems to prove margins, while maintenance follows rigorous schedules. Airports manage flow, rescue, de-icing and runways with clear procedures. The results are measured in punctuality, regularity and a very high level of safety, achieved by the addition of thousands of small gestures well done. Air travel then becomes an ordinary, precise act, where you move from one city to another like turning the page of an atlas. Behind this apparent simplicity lies a century of patient learning, international cooperation and engineering in the service of the same dream: to connect people quickly, safely and widely.

7.2 - Airports, terminals and passenger flows

An airport functions like a small, specialized city, where everything flows in a specific direction. Two worlds exist side by side: the city side, where the public is welcomed, and the airside, where flight operations take place. The runways and taxiways guide the planes, while the tower manages take-off and landing priorities. The terminal organizes passenger and baggage paths, with access controls clearly separating safe zones. Screens, announcements and signs unify information to avoid hesitation. Behind the glass, teams assign each flight to a gate, check the availability of a parking stand and coordinate buses, walkways and stairways. This arrangement transforms a varied crowd into legible queues that move forward in stages. The rule is simple: reduce unnecessary crossovers, keep margins, and keep aircraft, crew, passengers and baggage moving in parallel. Thanks to this choreography, a terminal becomes a large, efficient funnel to the sky.

For a passenger, the journey follows a series of successive doors. You enter the concourse, check in at a counter or kiosk, then hand over your hold baggage. Next comes the security check, where items are screened and electronic devices and liquids are separated according to the rules in force. For international flights, border control checks documents, while dedicated corridors direct passengers according to their destination. The boarding area features stores, water and seats near the gates, with line-up announcements to speed up boarding. Assistance lanes are available for families, people with reduced mobility and accompanied minors. Connections are equipped with signposted corridors to enable passengers to quickly join another flight without leaving the protected area. At every stage, the aim is clarity: visible information, identifiable staff, organized queues and reasonable waiting times. This legibility reduces stress and smoothes the entire flow.

The baggage process follows a hidden but rigorous network. After labelling at the counter or kiosk, a conveyor belt takes the bag to automated controls, then to a sorting machine which reads the barcode or a chip. Tilting or cross-belt systems direct each piece of luggage to the right flight. Bulky items pass through special circuits. For safety reasons, a matching system ensures that no suitcase boards without its owner. On long-haul flights, baggage is often placed in standardized containers to speed up loading. On arrival, the opposite occurs: unloading in the hold, internal transport, then carousel in the delivery hall. Oversized items go to a dedicated counter. On connecting flights, the sorting system immediately transfers to the second aircraft, with no need to go back to the city side. This network operates to the rhythm of schedules, priorities and unforeseen events, with teams ready to search for, retag and reroute overdue baggage so that it can be reunited with its owner.

Around the aircraft, a ground rotation resembles a timed ballet. A ramp agent guides you to the location, chocks immobilize the wheels, a gangway or stairway lands at the door. Unnecessary engine boost is cut off, and a ground power supply and pre-conditioned air are connected to save fuel. At the same time, the refuelling department supplies the truck or hydrant network, the catering department loads meals and drinking water, and other vehicles collect waste water. Baggage, freight and mail are stowed in the cargo holds according to a balanced stowage plan. On board, the crew carry out technical checks, quick cleaning, safety counts and cabin preparation. When everything is ready, the aircraft is cleared for departure, the doors are closed, the tractor spins and taxiing begins towards the holding point. In winter, a de-icing zone removes any ice before power-up. This compact sequence saves precious minutes and guarantees a safe departure.

Regulating airport capacity requires rules shared by airlines, air traffic control and the operator. Time slots limit arrivals and departures at peak times to avoid saturation. Platforms organized as hubs concentrate "waves" for short connections, with gates grouped by zone. Runway configuration adapts to wind and visibility, changing trajectories and taxiing times. Low-visibility procedures add prudent spacing when fog is inviting. A collaborative program, often referred to as a shared operational decision, synchronizes scheduled departure times, gate availability, crew readiness, fuel loading and runway threshold queues. This shared vision reduces engine-on waits and improves punctuality. Standardized departure and arrival itineraries smooth the flow in the air and guide you towards the final destination. Every coordinated minute on the ground is then gained in regularity in the sky.

Today's terminal seeks simplicity, accessibility and sober practices. Clear signage, glare-free lighting, plenty of seating and a step-free route help everyone, including those who need more time. Easy connections are supported by integrated rail and bus links to reduce the need for car journeys. On the track side, electric vehicles, fixed-feed walkways and waste separation reduce noise and emissions. Noise-reduction routes distribute take-offs over less sensitive areas, while ensuring safety. Passengers also contribute to fluidity by preparing documents, respecting baggage instructions and following the display. On the scale of a day, thousands of small coordinated actions transform a highly complex area into a serene journey. Understanding this orchestration makes you want to look behind the scenes and, why not, work on it one day, to help entire cities come together intelligently.

7.3 - Air traffic control and air routes

Air traffic control is the art of organizing flight paths so that large numbers of aircraft can share the same sky in safety. Its mission can be summed up in three verbs: separate, inform, rescue. There are three main positions. The airfield tower manages runways and taxiways, authorizes take-offs and landings, and looks after vehicles on the ground. The approach, around the city, orchestrates departures and arrivals, aligns aircraft on the correct runway and applies published slopes and headings. The en-route center, often called ACC, monitors cruise flights in large sectors, such as sky regions. Controllers see radar or ADS-B spots, listen to the radio and decide on vertical, lateral or longitudinal deviations. Minimums define the distances to be respected, e.g. a thousand feet vertically in RVSM space, or several nautical miles depending on the radar. Behind each clearance lies a simple reasoning: plan the trajectory, create a margin, then check that it remains intact when wind and speed change.

A controlled flight begins on the ground with a flight plan: departure, planned route, levels, duration and fuel. On take-off, the aircraft follows a standardized procedure, the SID, which plots headings and altitudes for a clean departure. En route, it uses RNAV routes or airways, and changes frequency at each sector boundary. At each handover, the next controller confirms the radar identification, assigns an altitude and heading, and sometimes a speed to maintain separation. The transponder responds to interrogations from the secondary radar with a "squawk" code; in Mode S and ADS-B, it even broadcasts the ID and calculated position. On arrival, a STAR guides you towards the city, then the approach aligns you on the final axis. All this is expressed in brief phraseology: "cleared climb level 180", "heading 240", "maintain 220 knots". Behind the words, a logic: divide space into legible slices, then hand over to the autopilot or manual pilot to fly the exact profile.

Air routes are like invisible highways, marked by five-letter points called waypoints: LGL, ABNIS, RONEX, etc. They are flown at flight levels, FL, which express altitude in hundreds of feet above the standard setting. For simplicity's sake, rules assign even or odd levels according to direction of travel, and RVSM allows a vertical separation of just 1,000 feet between FL290 and FL410, thanks to more precise altimetry. Lateral and longitudinal separation can be managed by radar distance, time between two points, or imposed speeds. With modern RNAV, many regions are adopting "Free Route Airspace": above a ceiling, points can be connected directly without following a rigid track, saving fuel and time. Crews also choose an optimum level according to weight and wind, then climb by "step climb" as the aircraft lightens. Less zigzagging, more efficiency, but the same discipline.

When the skies fill up, upstream organization prevents traffic jams. Flow management, or ATFM, calculates departure slots to stagger arrivals. En route, the centers fine-tune the spacing by small adjustments to heading or speed: "maintain 250 knots", "reduce to 220". On approach, aircraft are sequenced like pearls: RNAV trajectories, published holding patterns, then gradual integration onto the route. Modern techniques, such as Point Merge and Required Time of Arrival, adjust the length of the downwind leg so that each aircraft intercepts the final leg without stopping for long periods on the racetrack. If the weather's right, continuous descents save fuel and noise. Everyone wins: less braking, fewer go-arounds, smoother approaches. This music requires precise listening and sharp responses; each short instruction transforms a large flying crowd into a smooth, predictable file.

Over oceans and vast regions, radar is not always available. This is called oceanic space, with flexible routes that change daily according to jet streams. In the North Atlantic, tracks are published to take advantage of the westerly winds in the morning and easterly winds at night. Crews receive a clearance by HF radio or CPDLC data link, then report their positions at agreed points. Separation is by time and altitude, and route, Mach speed and fuel are monitored with particular rigor . Technologies such as ADS-C automatically send reports at intervals, while GPS provides highly accurate navigation. In the event of unforeseen circumstances, standard diversion and lateral deviation procedures protect other traffic. This remote navigation resembles an expedition: carefully prepared, following the plan, and keeping clear margins so that everyone crosses a blue desert in complete safety.

Air traffic control is constantly evolving, with more precision and less radio clutter. Digital towers use high-definition cameras to remotely monitor isolated runways. Data exchanges, CPDLC and "digital clearances", reduce listening errors and free up frequency. Satellite ADS-B extends surveillance over the oceans, while performance-based navigation, PBN, enables smoother, shorter profiles. Many regions are introducing "Free Route" and continuous descents to save fuel and noise. Yet the basics remain the same: a clear plan, brief instructions, cross-checking between crew and controller. The day you take the controls, you'll follow the same method: prepare, announce, fly precisely, correct early. This shared choreography transforms a vast sky into a cooperative network.

Knowing how it works makes you want to respect it, progress in it, and perhaps one day work in it to guide others.

7.4 - Crew roles and operations

Behind every successful flight lies an entire team orchestrating dozens of actions at just the right moment. In the cockpit, the pilot-in-command decides and the co-pilot executes, sharing tasks to keep a watchful eye. In the cabin, cabin crew ensure safety and comfort, pay attention to passengers and apply precise procedures. On the ground, ground staff manage doors, gangways and baggage, while mechanics monitor the aircraft's health. In a discreet center called operations, dispatchers draw up the flight plan and monitor the aircraft on map and screen like guardian angels. Everyone speaks the same language: clear procedures, checklists, radio phraseology, and a culture called CRM where everyone says what they see and dares to point out any doubts. This teamwork transforms a complex piece of equipment into a reliable service, where the right move by each individual reinforces the safety of all.

The day begins long before passengers arrive at the terminal. Operations gather weather, winds aloft, NOTAMs and runway conditions, then calculate an efficient route with the necessary fuel plus reserves. The pilot-in-command checks weight and balance from a document called a loadsheet, considers take-off distance according to temperature and wind conditions, and validates the de-icing plan if weather conditions dictate. A minimum equipment list, the MEL, authorizes flight even if a non-essential accessory is temporarily unavailable, provided certain limits are respected. In the crew briefing, ideas are lined up: runway, initial heading, altitudes, daily threats and a plan if something goes wrong. Roles are allocated, frequencies, charts and performance are prepared, and then we go into a "sterile cockpit" to banish all distractions during critical phases. This preparation makes the rest easier: everyone knows what to do and when.

Around the aircraft, the ground rotation resembles a regulated ballet. The pilot performs the pre-flight check, hand and eye on flaps, tires, cowlings and probes, while the crew load cargo and galley according to a balanced plan. The cabin crew count passengers, check seats, vests and exits, then prepare for the safety demonstration. At boarding, each door is armed and then "cross-checked", double-checking to avoid any mistakes. When everything is ready, the doors are closed, the taxi clearance is received, and the tractor pushes the aircraft to safety under the signals of the ramp agents. The pilots follow the checklist, start the engines, test the control surfaces and systems, then taxi to the holding point. Everyone keeps an eye on their own bubble: on the ground, they remain attentive to markings, traffic and instructions from the tower. This calm choreography avoids haste and transforms a busy parking lot into a clean, controlled departure.

In flight, the crew becomes energy and route guardians. One pilot "holds" the plane, monitoring attitude, speed and navigation; the other manages the radio, systems and calculations. Automation helps, but awareness remains: understanding which mode is active and what the plane is going to do in the next ten seconds. Levels and headings are adjusted according to the control, fuel consumption is optimized, the weather is monitored and hectic areas are avoided. In the cabin, cabin crew keep an eye on what matters: passengers who are uncomfortable, turbulence to be avoided, equipment to be secured. In the event of the unexpected, one method is applied: identify, communicate, decide. A technical problem is dealt with by means of abnormal checklists, consultation with operations and the choice of a credible diversion. A momentary malaise triggers a medical kit, a call to the ground doctor and a search for the most suitable airfield. In all cases, the objective remains the same: a safe and clear arrival.

The approach combines preparation and precision. Before descending, the crew briefs the pilot on the chosen procedure, its altitudes, minimums and any go-arounds. The cabin crew "prepare the cabin", making sure everything is stowed and secured, then sit down for the landing. Pilots follow a STAR, intercepting the axis and slope, stabilizing speed and configuration at a published height, and keeping a margin for unforeseen circumstances. If the trajectory is not clean, a go-around is decided without hesitation: better a lap than a forced landing. After landing, we clear the runway, announce "runway clear", then taxi to the gate, respecting ground markings and instructions. At standstill, engines off, belts held to signal, doors disarmed and gateway connected. All these steps are simple when you know them; together, they transform a well-mannered final into a safe and peaceful arrival.

The flight doesn't end with the engines shutting down. Then come the debriefing, the technical logbook update and, if necessary, a maintenance message for a faulty light or vibration. Operations compare planned and actual routes, noting wind and fuel consumption to improve future plans. Safety progresses thanks to feedback in a system called SMS, where we declare without punishment to learn collectively. Ongoing training is the lifeblood of our crews, with simulators for rare breakdowns, training in precision approaches and regular line checks. Fatigue management organizes schedules with sufficient rest, because a rested crew makes better decisions. Finally, attention to the environment is growing: taxiing on a single engine whenever possible, ground power supply rather than auxiliary power, continuous descent profiles. This preparation-execution-improvement loop builds a discreet reliability, thanks to which millions of trips go ahead as planned, with calm and confidence.

7.5 - Maintenance, reliability and line safety

In an airline, maintenance is the backbone of reliability. It serves three simple purposes: prevention, repair and improvement. Prevention means inspecting before a fault occurs. Repairing means putting a system back into working order quickly and efficiently. Improving means analyzing data to make the aircraft more robust. Airworthiness is the official assurance that the aircraft complies with technical regulations and can fly safely. Around the aircraft, a team coordinates these tasks day and night: ramp mechanics, engineers, logisticians and airworthiness managers. The cockpit and the workshop talk to each other constantly, as the slightest clue may reveal a setting that needs fine-tuning. The visible objective for passengers is punctuality; the hidden but essential objective is departure reliability, the ability to leave on time with a fully safe aircraft. This result is not the result of luck, but of a meticulous method, repeated at every stopover and after every flight.

Maintenance is organized in complementary layers. As close as possible to operations, line maintenance checks the aircraft at every stop: levels, tires, sight glasses, leaks, minor replacements. Daily and weekly inspections complete this first net. More in-depth, scheduled hangar visits open cowlings and panels, check structures, systems and cabins, and test ice protection, brakes and controls. The so-called "heavy visits" immobilize the aircraft for longer periods to measure the wear and tear of major components and apply manufacturer's instructions. Each task follows a precise sheet, with calibrated tools and defined tightening torques. Nothing is left to chance: traceable parts, adapted products, cross-checks. Before the machine is put back into service, a ground test is carried out, and sometimes a check flight. This tiered organization ensures that small details are seen often, and large ones regularly, so that the aircraft remains sound throughout its career.

Modern reliability is born of data. The aircraft records temperatures, vibrations, pressures and events, which are then passed on to technical operations. Maintenance computers signal a faulty sensor, a weakening pump or a slow engine start-up. Engineers follow trends: a slow drift warns of a breakdown. We then replace a part at a chosen moment, on an equipped basis, rather than waiting for the unexpected stop. Engines are closely monitored through oil analysis, efficiency measurements and in-flight data transmission. Reliability-oriented methods, derived from a function-based maintenance logic, help decide what to check and when. Logistics follow: calculated inventories, rotating repair parts, approved workshops. In this way, maintenance becomes predictive as well as corrective. The practical result: fewer contingencies, better fleet availability and constant passenger comfort, because the aircraft leaves ready, with its systems checked and its technical reserves under control.

Safety depends not just on tools, but on a shared culture. Companies apply a safety management system, in which an event is reported without blame, so as to learn collectively. Quality audits verify procedures, documents and practices on a daily basis. Ongoing training maintains skills: new instructions, new materials, training for unusual interventions. Technical and flight crews review operating scenarios together, so that everyone understands the impact of their actions on others. Flight analysis programs transform anonymized parameters into ideas for improvement: approach too fast, aggressive braking, poorly anticipated turbulence. The cabin is also involved: safety equipment is checked, validity dates are monitored, and demonstrations are meticulous. This common attitude is based on three simple reflexes: signal early, cross-check, correct calmly. It transforms a large organization into an attentive team capable of preventing rather than suffering.

Operating a flight without all possible accessories is sometimes acceptable, but never without rules. The minimum equipment list specifies what can be temporarily unavailable and under what conditions: weather limitations, altitudes, duration, repair times. The logic is clear: many functions are redundant, so we can leave if safety remains fully assured, while planning for rapid correction. On certain long-haul routes, additional requirements apply to ensure prudent autonomy and credible diversions. In such cases, the aircraft receives enhanced pre-departure checks, as well as careful en-route monitoring of parameters. This responsible approach avoids grounding for a non-critical detail, while protecting the safety margin. As for the crew, they are kept precisely informed of the technical status and adapt their briefings accordingly. The important thing is not to have everything perfect, but to have understood, documented and mastered everything before driving.

Line safety is also at stake on the ground, minute by minute. Around the aircraft, we check that there are no objects that could be sucked up, we ground the aircraft during refuelling, and we keep clear zones during push-back. In winter, de-icing removes snow and ice that would increase drag and reduce lift. In the cab, check exits, vests and fire extinguishers, and stow equipment securely. On taxi, markings, lights and visual guidance reduce the risk of error; on final, warning systems monitor trajectory and proximity to the ground. Airports inspect runways, measure grip and adjust spacing in case of reduced visibility. At every stage, one idea remains: punctuality yes, but never without margins. It's this blend of anticipation, method and coordination that enables thousands of daily flights to arrive serenely. Understanding this human and technical mechanism makes us want to respect it and, perhaps, contribute to it one day.

Chapter 8: Special Missions and Rescue

8.1 - Military aviation, hunting and training

Military aviation protects a country's skies, looks far ahead and supports other forces when necessary. Hunting is the branch that reacts quickly, identifies unknown aircraft and guides civilian aircraft in difficulty if necessary. Many missions are preventive and visible on a day-to-day basis: alert patrols, "sky policing" around airports, escorting a flight that no longer responds to the radio. Each action follows precise rules, with a decision-making chain and specialized air traffic control. We speak of procedure rather than improvisation: flight plan, authorized zones, altitudes, recorded communications. Crews also apply air law and international rules governing the use of force. On the ground, weather, operations and maintenance teams monitor the parameters that can delay departure. This organization transforms a rapid take-off into a controlled gesture, where speed counts as much as caution, to keep the skies safe and clear for all.

A fighter plane aims for three qualities: far vision, strong maneuvering and safe return. To see far, it brings together complementary sensors: radar to detect, infrared sensors to sense heat, data links to share the situation with allies. To maneuver, it has a light, solid airframe, fly-by-wire electric controls that help keep it stable when the wing is working hard, and a good thrust-to-weight ratio. Some fly safely past Mach 1, others prefer autonomy and versatility. Well-known examples include the agile and compact F-16, the air-superiority-oriented Eurofighter Typhoon, and the Dassault Rafale, which is designed for a wide range of missions. Radar discretion depends on shapes and materials that "reflect" fewer waves than a simple geometry. Additional tanks, sensor pods and training equipment can be fitted under the wing. The objective remains the same: to provide a highly responsive, reliable tool, capable of acting without startling other users of the sky.

Training to become a military pilot is a long and progressive process. After medical and psycho-technical selection, students first learn about safety, radio and the basics of flying a propeller-driven training aircraft, such as a Pilatus PC-21 or a T-6. Here, we work on attitude, coordinated turns, simple navigation and clean landing. Then comes the "advanced" phase on a training jet, such as a BAE Hawk, T-45 or M-346, where we discover high speeds, energy management and complex procedures. Simulators play a central role: difficult weather conditions, rare breakdowns, crew coordination - everything is rehearsed to the point of reflex. At the same time, courses in aerodynamics, meteorology, human factors and aeronautical English round out the technical aspects. The final stage is called operational transformation: you join a squadron and learn about the mission aircraft, its sensors, fuel management and methods. At each stage, briefings and debriefings monitor progress with measurable criteria.

On the tactical side, the key is situational awareness: knowing who is where, at what altitude, and with what intention. In patrols, two or four aircraft fly in formation to cover each other. Energy is managed like treasure: speed, altitude and trajectories determine the ability to maneuver cleanly. Crews learn simple geometries to intercept without surprise, keep a safe distance from civilian traffic, and retain the option of abandoning if weather or fuel become limiting. Ground radars and AWACS sometimes guide the patrol to the right area, like a moving beacon. In-flight refuelling extends endurance as the mission stretches. International exercises serve as a life-size school: common procedures, clear phraseology, shared rules of engagement. The method is always the same: prepare, execute, check; then improve during debriefing thanks to flight recordings.

A successful mission depends as much on the ground crews as on the pilots. Mechanics ensure the fleet's availability: inspections, preventive changes, run-up tests. Systems specialists look after sensors, software and data links. Planners build the flight dossier: weather, NOTAMs, routes, fuel, altitudes, active zones, time slots. The runway safety team checks runway lighting, the presence of birds and the cleanliness of manoeuvring areas. While the aircraft is taxiing, technicians monitor temperatures, pressures and any maintenance messages. These logistics are based on traced inventories, calibrated tools and written procedures. After landing, a technical report signals the slightest vibration or doubtful indication, so that it can be dealt with before the next flight. The whole process resembles a relay: each gesture prepares the next. When everything is aligned, a squadron can keep alert for weeks on end, with regular departures and measured reliability.

Behind performance lie ethics and human preparation. Crews train in centrifuge load factors and wear anti-g suits to stay clear-headed during maneuvers. Fatigue management, hydration and concentration are learned as much as piloting. Strict identification and safety rules are observed, especially near civilian roads, and the precautionary principle is applied when in doubt. Careers are varied: fighter pilot, systems navigator-officer, air defense controller, mechanic, engineer, meteorologist. Everyone shares the same culture: speak plainly, cross-check, decide on time. Exchanges with other air forces develop interoperability and technical humility. In the final analysis, military aviation is not just about speed; it's a school of method and responsibility. It shows that we can combine self-control, science and teamwork to protect and serve, keeping the skies clear and safe for all.

8.2 - Strategic airlift and supply

Strategic airlift is the great highway of the skies, rapidly linking far-flung points with heavy equipment, teams and humanitarian aid. The term "strategic" is used when it is necessary to cross continents; "tactical" is used for shorter hops to more modest locations, close to the action or difficult to reach. These missions build air bridges, a series of regular flights capable of sustaining an operation for weeks on end. They move field hospitals, engineering vehicles, generators and supplies, sometimes to rudimentary airstrips. Reliability is key: schedules kept, aircraft available, coordination with air traffic control and local authorities. A well-chosen stopover serves as a relay point for fuel, crews and maintenance. This work resembles a giant logistics chain where every link counts: planning, loading, flight, unloading, return. Thanks to this method, a requirement spotted on a map quickly becomes pallets placed in the right place, ready for use.

Transport aircraft are a family of complementary talents. The C-5 Galaxy and the An-124 carry "outsize" loads such as helicopters or infrastructure components. The C-17 Globemaster III combines a large payload with short-landing capability, useful on robust but limited runways. The A400M Atlas plays the role of Swiss Army knife, with its substantial load, decent range and suitability for rough terrain, while the C-130 Hercules remains the benchmark for tactical transport, sometimes equipped with skis for polar zones. Inside, the cargo compartment is equipped with standard 463L pallets, rails and lashing points to speed loading and stowage. Rear ramps facilitate the loading of roll-on/roll-off vehicles. Loading gliders, winches and motorized carts save precious minutes. Every flight complies with the maximum weight, centering and certified securing requirements, as a poorly secured pallet can move during take-off or braking. Properly prepared, the cargo hold becomes a solid puzzle that can be moved quickly.

Planning transforms the scope of a mission into concrete steps. Dispatchers compare weather, winds aloft and NOTAMs, choose RNAV routes and request diplomatic overflight clearances. Take-off slots, parking, fuel and handling crews are booked at the stopover. Loadmasters calculate weight and balance, install nets, straps and tie-down bars, and check hazardous materials according to regulations. Pilots study take-off performance, climb gradients and credible alternates. In remote areas, a forward base serves as a hub to consolidate freight and personnel before final distribution in smaller aircraft. During an aid operation, priorities are ranked: water purifiers, tents, rations, heat-sensitive medicines in refrigerated containers. Everything is documented: packing lists, temperatures, seals. This rigor creates trust between civilian and military actors. On arrival, a timed unloading operation is followed by local distribution to ensure that the aid quickly becomes useful.

In-flight refuelling extends the reach of non-stop missions. Two systems coexist. The rigid boom, controlled by an operator from the rear of the KC-135, KC-10 or KC-46, quickly transfers a large flow to compatible aircraft. The "basket-pipe" nacelle of the A330 MRTT, A400M or under-wing pods offers ideal flexibility for many aircraft equipped with a fixed boom. The rendezvous takes place on dedicated routes, known as refueling runways, with published altitudes, separations and frequencies. Day or night, sometimes with night vision binoculars, the receiver reaches a stable position, follows the feeder's luminous cues, then initiates the connection. The handover monitors pressures, flow rates and remaining fuel. At the end, we separate according to a set pattern. This capability avoids detours, reduces sensitive stopovers and means that you can arrive "on the spot" with generous autonomy to complete your planned mission without rushing back.

Safe refuelling relies on precise roles and proven procedures. The receiver pilot holds a position a few meters away, gently corrects with rudder and stick, and announces any drift. The boom operator or refueling manager monitors alignment, structural load and automatic cut-off in case of jerks. Key words trigger immediate separation if one of the two crews is not satisfied; the breakaway maneuver quickly clears space, with each crew following a known trajectory. Respecting weather limits avoids flying into too much turbulence. Checklists cover lighting, pressurization, anti-icing and fuel management, so that final weight and balance remain compatible with the rest of the flight. Progressive training takes place in the simulator, followed by real flights, day and night, in a variety of conditions. This pedagogy creates calm automatisms, indispensable when precision is measured in meters and knots.

Strategic transport and refueling serve more than just deployments: they support peace operations, scheduled medical evacuations, humanitarian airlifts and far-flung scientific missions, even on snow-covered slopes with ski-equipped aircraft. They bring generators, communication stations and rescue teams, then leave with equipment to be repaired. Each rotation is a sequence of planning, execution and improvement, based on feedback and technical data. Modern fleets combine reliable avionics, efficient engines and planned maintenance to keep on schedule. Crews apply the same grammar as in civil aviation: clear briefings, checklists, phraseology, CRM. This combination of logistics and precision saves time where it counts most. To learn how it works is to discover another facet of aviation: one that connects fast, far and good, to make possible what seemed out of reach.

8.3 - Rescue helicopters and evacuations

Rescue helicopters turn minutes into extra opportunities by rapidly linking a hard-to-reach location to an equipped hospital. Their missions vary: medical evacuation from an isolated road, assistance in the mountains, recovery at sea, transfer between specialized hospitals. All around them, a network of bases stand watch day and night, with ready crews and preheated machines. On board are usually a pilot, a winch technician or cargo operator, and a medical team comprising one or two flight-trained medical staff. Before each departure, a briefing covers trajectory, weather, terrain and fuel. En route, the radio connects the coordination center, ground services and the receiving hospital. Piloting follows a golden rule: stability, visibility, margin. The helicopter invites itself in where the road is slow or absent, then leaves as soon as the situation has stabilized. This precise mobility is not improvised: it's based on procedures, rigorous maintenance and seamless cooperation between land, sky and hospital.

These aircraft combine measured power with finesse. Most are twin-engined, to guarantee good performance in the event of a failure on one unit. Modern rotors, sometimes protected by a tail window, reduce noise and improve safety close to the ground. Avionics include a precise autopilot, digital charts, night vision, multiple radios and sometimes instrument guidance. The cabin is designed as a small treatment room: lockable stretcher, tie-down rails, medical power supply, oxygen, discreet lighting. A cable winch enables the helicopter to be hoisted over a cliff or roof when there is no landing area. Performance is calculated for each mission: weight, temperature, altitude and obstacles dictate power and hover margin. The rotor blast, known as rotorwash, raises dust, snow or pebbles, hence the need for a gentle approach and a careful choice of axis and height. The objective is always the same: a clean landing, a safe take-off, preserving crew and patient.

On intervention, the pilot looks for a suitable landing area. The preferred site is flat, clear, far from power lines and large enough for the rotor disk. In urban areas, a crossroads or a sports field may be suitable, provided the authorities secure the perimeter. In the countryside, avoid tall grass and rolling stones; in dust or snow, keep the drive slow to maintain visual reference points. A contact person on the ground helps by describing wind, obstacles and ground conditions, then keeps curious onlookers at a distance. If the area is too narrow, the winch takes over: the operator stabilizes the cabin, the rescuer descends, secures it, then coordinates the ascent. On arrival at the hospital, a helipad receives the aircraft, with beaconing, firefighting and fast-tracking to services. At night, the crew wears night-vision binoculars and follows discreet beaconing to avoid glare. Every gesture is simple, but order counts.

The mountains and the sea call for special skills. At altitude, the "lighter" air reduces lift; the heat accentuates this effect, making it necessary to take care with mass margins and approaches. The wind accelerates on the ridges, swirls in the valleys, and can trap a hover if you don't keep your own speed. Crews are trained to fly on slopes, to spot rollers and to land on soft snow where the aircraft risks sinking. At sea, the surface moves, reflects and deceives; illusions are avoided by keeping stable landmarks and clear altitudes. An onboard swimmer can join a dinghy, secure and then guide the winch. Vessels cooperate by offering a stable heading and a favorable relative wind. Whether it's a gusty peak or a long swell, the recipe remains the same: fine reading of the environment, short communication, gentle corrections and rapid decision-making if the margin decreases.

Onboard medicine is organized to provide care on the move. The cabin houses monitors, oxygen, portable aspirators, ventilators, infusions and protective equipment. Caregivers stabilize, monitor and communicate with the receiving hospital to prepare the patient for reception in a suitable ward. The helicopter then becomes a gateway to a useful technical platform. Gestures are carried out attached, with equipment secured, as safety is paramount during dynamic phases. Boarding follows a set sequence: stretcher locked, sensors connected, hoses secured, belts fastened, doors checked. In flight, checklists punctuate the steps, while the radio transmits estimated arrival times and special needs. On landing, the team reaches the dedicated elevators in just a few minutes. This coordination transforms speed into efficiency: a short but controlled journey enables the hospital to prepare rooms and specialists, and the crew to remain focused on the essentials, i.e. continuous, serene care.

Behind precision lie training, maintenance and the human factor. Crews regularly practice rare breakdowns, marginal weather management and night-time procedures in simulators. Autorotation training provides reflexes for dealing with power loss. Maintenance follows strict schedules, from winch checks to blade inspections, to ensure that the aircraft maintains its performance. Before each mission, a risk assessment sets clear limits: if visibility drops or the wind exceeds thresholds, we postpone or adapt. After the mission, a debriefing notes what went well and what can be improved: landing area, radio link, route, stowage. The environment also counts: noise-reduction trajectories near dwellings, safety of local residents, educating witnesses to keep the landing area clear. This calm, demanding culture shows that a rescue helicopter is not just fast; it is above all precise, thoughtful and deeply collective.

8.4 - Drones, surveillance and mapping

Drones, also known as unmanned aerial vehicles (UAVs), are small aircraft without an onboard pilot, carrying sensors for observation and measurement. Two main families dominate: multi-rotors capable of hovering, and durable fixed-wing aircraft that cover large areas. On board, an autopilot reads an inertial unit, a GNSS receiver, a compass and often a barometric altimeter; it stabilizes the aircraft and follows a flight plan. A gimbal isolates the camera from vibrations to keep the horizon straight. The radio link controls, displays telemetry and triggers shots. The battery provides the power, hence the importance of weight and balance. This flying toolbox can be used to inspect, map, monitor, rescue or count living creatures without getting too close. Because they fly low and slow, drones see details invisible from a plane. The secret is in the method: choosing the right type of aircraft, preparing a safe trajectory, setting up sensors and security, then transforming the images into useful information.

Images become measurements, thanks to the right sensors. An RGB camera produces sharp photos for orthophoto and 3D models; a multispectral camera observes several visible and near-infrared bands to estimate crop vigor and humidity; a thermal camera locates heat loss or hot spots on solar panels. LiDAR emits laser pulses and measures the return time to build a georeferenced point cloud. A stabilized gimbal guards the axis during gusts. Ground control points improve planimetric and altimetric accuracy; RTK or PPK corrects GNSS position in real time or after the event. Aperture, ISO and shutter speed are set to avoid blur, reference panels are calibrated in multispectral, and focus is checked on-screen. On a structure, we choose definition and plan tight orbits. On a territory, we fly higher, with parallel lines to ensure wide coverage.

Photogrammetry reconstructs relief from overlapping photos. The telepilot prepares a checkerboard pattern with longitudinal and lateral overlap, sets altitude, speed and orientation, then chooses lighting without harsh shadows. The height determines the size of the pixel on the ground, known as the GSD: the higher you fly, the finer the detail. After the flight, a software program aligns the shots by detecting common points, calculates the virtual camera and generates a dense point cloud. The result is a perspective-free orthomosaic, a digital surface model, and sometimes a digital terrain model if vegetation is separated. These products are used to measure surfaces, excavation volumes, building heights, slopes and runoff. In agriculture, spectral indices help identify stressed areas; in archaeology, discrete reliefs appear; in urban planning, facades are modeled to study sunlight. Each step requires rigor: good geolocation, sufficient coverage, calibrated sensors and quality controls to guarantee an accurate, usable map.

Drone surveillance allows us to observe quickly and closely, without exposing our teams. Power lines can be traversed by following waypoints, roofs can be checked without a gondola, dikes photographed after a flood, pipelines monitored along mapped corridors. Wildlife counts are carried out at sufficient height to limit disturbance. These missions involve the handling of sensitive data: privacy is respected, the authorities are informed if necessary, and the data is stored carefully. Common rules often require direct line-of-sight flying, limited heights, a secure take-off zone and avoidance of crowds; beyond line-of-sight, authorization is required to manage the risk. Functions to protect the aircraft include geo-referencing, return-to-home in the event of a lost link, battery alarms and flight logs. The remote pilot remains in control of the environment: choice of axis to reduce noise, reasonable distance from people, postponement if the wind picks up. The quality of a useful flight depends as much on ethics as on technique.

A successful mission is the result of serious preparation. The remote pilot consults the weather forecast and NOTAMs, chooses a low-wind window and avoids rain and fog, which can mislead the sensors, IMU and altimeter. A checklist verifies propellers, tightenings, firmware, calibrated compass, balanced batteries, free storage and updated geographical databases. A spotter is on hand to keep an eye out for birds, lines and curious onlookers. On the ground, you choose a clear area, set up a take-off mat, announce your intentions and maintain an escape trajectory. During the flight, we check voltage, temperature, wind strength, link quality and satellites; at the slightest doubt, we simplify the mission and return to land.

Electronic identification devices make the aircraft visible to the authorities; registration and labelling facilitate traceability. After landing, the files are saved and clearly named, then a short report is written to help the next team go faster and safer.

Behind these precise flights lies a complete industry. Schools provide training in remote piloting, regulations and map reading; workshops maintain chassis, engines, propellers and gimbals; analysts transform pixels and dots into maps ready for decisions. Emergency services rely on mapping teams to quickly deliver orthomosaics of assessments, axis cross-sections, flooded rights-of-way and landslide volumes. Forest inventories identify regeneration and gaps, precision agriculture targets the right amount of water, and industrial inspections reduce work at height. Synchronized swarms create light shows or cover a sports field in minutes for an organized search. Each project respects local rules, protects data and documents methods to ensure reproducibility. This creative world brings together mechanics, geomaticians, naturalists and pilots around the same idea: observe to understand. By learning to plan, fly clean and read the maps produced, a reader can transform a flight into shared knowledge that helps the field.

8.5 - Firefighting and civil missions

Fighting a fire from the air saves time and margins for ground crews. Firefighting aviation doesn't "kill" fires on its own: it slows progress, protects homes, secures evacuation routes or reinforces support points. Around a fire, a command post coordinates meteorology, topography, access routes and priorities. Aerial observers describe the front, smoke columns, eddies and wind shifts. A strategy is then chosen: rapid initial attack, anchoring on a line, protecting a flank. Aircraft take off in series, each with a clear role and separate altitudes. One cycle follows another: water intake or retardant, transit, release, return to the resource. Safety always takes precedence: sufficient altitude, clear trajectories, planned clearance if smoke suddenly masks the area. This method transforms an emergency into a series of measured actions, with every minute gained bringing the fire closer to a controllable perimeter.

There are two main, complementary families of water-bombing aircraft. Amphibious aircraft "scoop" water from a lake or the sea, reload and return to the front line very quickly; they deposit water or a foaming additive that cools and wets vegetation. Converted airliners or turboprops, on the other hand, carry large quantities of red retardant; this viscous mixture is not designed to extinguish, but to create a barrier that slows the advance of the flames. An attack aircraft, sometimes called a coordinator, opens the route, locates the terrain, marks the axis with smoke and announces course, height and exit point. The drop is made low, at a steady speed, against the wind, to ensure that the jet spreads out correctly. The crew aims for a natural anchor, a road, a firebreak or a previously treated area, in order to close a door to the fire. Each pass is part of a plan shared with the ground teams, who consolidate immediately.

Helicopters provide precision. With a ventral tank or a pendulum bucket, they take on water in a matter of seconds and apply a highly targeted spray, useful near houses, pylons or on a fire still hidden by the terrain. Some carry a foam lance, while others deploy "helitack" teams who attack on foot and establish a line with chainsaws and shovels. The mission is organized from a heli-base, where fuel, maintenance, spare parts and crew rotations are managed. The pilot chooses a clean axis, avoids power lines and keeps speed to a minimum so as not to lose his bearings in the smoke. The powerful rotor blast means that curious onlookers have to be kept at a distance; on soft ground, approach gently to avoid raising a blinding cloud. At night, some fleets use night-vision binoculars according to strict rules. The aim is to strike fast and close, without ever surprising the ground teams.

Beyond firefighting, civil aviation carries out essential public missions that resemble logistical superpowers. Light aircraft map out the storm's aftermath to identify cut-off roads, landslides and damaged roofs; their multispectral cameras then help local authorities prioritize repairs. Maritime patrols monitor pollution, spot oil slicks, drift nets and wrecks, and guide assistance vessels. Crews parachute water, rations or radios to isolated teams, while medical aircraft rapidly transfer patients to specialized hospitals when helicopters are out of range. In winter, devices measure snow cover and help predict avalanches; in summer, they monitor reservoir levels. All use the same grammar: serious preparation , checklists, clear phraseology, weather read closely. The central idea remains unchanged: to fly in order to observe, locate, link and then transmit useful information to those on the ground.

To keep everything safe, the airspace around a fire is organized like a funnel. A coordinator manages altitudes: drop planes higher up on straight trajectories, helicopters lower down for precision, one-way traffic around a published entry and exit point. A dedicated frequency brings together pilots and commanders, with short, repeated messages. The risks are well known: opaque smoke, optical illusions over terrain, thermal turbulence, power lines, unauthorized drones. Crews are briefed on an escape plan and a height limit never to be exceeded. Logistics keep pace: water points, retardant bases, fuel, maintenance teams ready to change a hose or a caster. Technical hygiene counts: regular engine tests, release hatch inspections, filter cleaning. After each mission, a debriefing is held to share trajectories, wind effects and the quality of drops on the ground. This prepare-act-learn loop increases efficiency without ever reducing the safety margin.

These civilian missions show that aviation is patient, methodical and at the service of the common good. Before the summer, crews practice low-level navigation, smoky approaches and calibrated airdrops; local authorities clear brush, create water points and test sirens. When the alarm goes off, everyone takes up their role without hesitation. Aircraft set up protective barriers, helicopters drop teams, ground crews close the line, and observation aircraft report back to adjust the maneuver. After the crisis, aerial mapping helps restore forests, roads and networks. As you read these pages, you can already prepare yourself: learn about the weather, respect nature, know the emergency numbers, and take an interest in the sky and rescue professions. Science, prudence and team spirit take pride of place. To approach this knowledge is to participate in the collective energy that protects and rebuilds. Every gesture counts.

Chapter 9: Technologies and aeronautical revolutions

9.1 - Composite materials and lightweight structures

A composite material combines two ingredients to achieve more than each one separately: high-strength fibers and a resin that bonds and transmits forces. Carbon fibers offer remarkable strength and rigidity for low mass; glass fibers are economical; aramid fibers, such as Kevlar, resist impact well. Resin, often epoxy, maintains fiber orientation and protects against moisture. The result is anisotropic: very stiff along the fibers, softer elsewhere. In aircraft, this "directionality" allows the material to be placed where the load actually passes, saving precious kilos. For the same mass, a carbon panel can be several times stiffer than standard aluminum. Less mass means shorter take-offs, lower fuel consumption and more range. Modern gliders, today's airliners and many propellers already make use of these advantages. The key idea is simple to remember: to fly far, we hunt down every unnecessary gram without sacrificing strength.

To transform a thin skin into a solid structure, engineers love "sandwich" architecture. Imagine a rusk: two thin skins and "honey" in the middle. In aeronautics, this core is a honeycomb of aluminum or polymer, sometimes a technical foam. Composite skins bear the brunt of tension and compression; the core holds the gap, fights buckling and takes up shear. The result is a highly rigid panel with very little mass, perfect for floors, control surfaces, fairings or hoods. Careful attention is paid to the edges, as this is where the stresses are concentrated: solid reinforcements, inserts for screws and hinges. Under load, a sandwich deforms like a high but light beam. In the event of impact, it may crush locally: the area is then inspected to check that the core has not been delaminated. This recipe combines intelligent geometry and modern materials to produce surfaces that resist without becoming heavy.

Clean manufacturing requires appropriate processes. Draping involves laying fabric or uni-directional plies at selected angles , e.g. 0°, ±45°, 90°, then impregnating them with resin. Under vacuum, a tarpaulin compresses the stack; in the autoclave, pressure and heat drive out bubbles and voids to obtain a dense, regular part. Resin infusion uses vacuum to circulate resin through dry fibers, useful for large parts. Resin transfer molding (RTM) closes the fibers in a mold and then injects them, producing dimensionally stable parts. Thermoplastic composites, heated then welded, promise faster repairs and easier recycling. Whatever you choose, quality depends on control: fabric humidity, polymerization temperature, fiber content, ply alignment. A faulty pleat or an air pocket can weaken an entire area. Manufacturing is therefore as much about chemistry as it is about meticulous sewing.

Designing in composite means writing a score of angles. Folds at 0° carry the elongation, those at ±45° bind the structure in shear, and those at 90° hold the width. The order of layers and symmetry prevent warping. Local reinforcements are added near fasteners, rails and frames to guide forces. On the risk side, a blow can loosen folds: this is called delamination. This is tracked by non-destructive testing, such as ultrasound, thermography or a simple "tap test" that listens to the part. Lightning strikes require a fine metal mesh under the paint to guide the current without damaging the fibers. Repairs are carried out by "scarifying" a gentle slope, then re-bonding folds according to the original plan and vacuum-polymerizing. The golden rule remains damage tolerance: dimensioning so that a reasonable impact does not prevent the aircraft from completing its flight and landing safely.

In an aircraft, composite is not alone: it cooperates with metals and fasteners. Aluminum remains king for certain areas that are not very hot and easy to repair; titanium shines near high temperatures, around engines and leading edges that are subject to stress. These worlds are linked by structural bonding and bolting. Bonding distributes forces and avoids drilling too many holes; bolting provides visible security and useful disassembly. Carbon and aluminum are electrically insulated to prevent galvanic corrosion. Large modern wings, glider hulls, many propellers and rotor blades already exploit these hybrids. The same philosophy applies to interiors: sandwich bulkheads and floors can better support cabin loads, while weighing less. This material-process-design cooperation goes hand in hand with demanding certification that checks fatigue, impact resistance, fire behavior and repairability, so that lightness is never a gamble, but a proof.

Then there's the question of life cycle. Thermosetting resins are still difficult to recycle: fibers are recovered, but the chain can be improved. Thermoplastics are making progress, as they can be re-welded and better reprocessed. New avenues are emerging: bio-sourced resins, flax or basalt fibers for certain secondary parts, and less energy-intensive processes. At the same time, the "health" of structures is monitored by sensors: fiber-optic networks measure deformations and warn of the onset of cracking; vibration analysis identifies loosening. Digital tools, such as finite element analysis and computer-aided manufacturing, help to place materials and reinforcements precisely. The ambition remains the same: lighter, safer and more durable. For a young reader, the image to remember is that of a giant scientific origami, made of oriented layers, clever glue and organized air, transforming black fabrics into solid wings. Well-thought-out lightness becomes an engine of efficiency.

9.2 - Turbojets, turboprops and blowers

A turbojet, a turboprop and a fan are three ways of using the same idea: the gas turbine. Air is swallowed, compressed, mixed with fuel, ignited, then expelled aft. The reaction pushes the aircraft forward. The difference lies in the way this energy is used. The pure turbojet accelerates a small flow of air very quickly: ideal for very fast flight. The turboprop diverts most of the power to a propeller, which accelerates a large volume of air, but slowly: unbeatable at low and medium speeds. The fan, or turbofan, combines the two: a large "wheel" at the front, the fan, propels a cold flow around the hot core, giving plenty of thrust with less noise and fuel. The architecture is chosen according to the mission: short take-off, long travel, high flight, high speed. Understanding this trio means understanding how to transform heat into motion with maximum efficiency.

At the heart of these engines, four main components work in a chain: compressor, combustion chamber, turbine and nozzle. The compressor, either axial or centrifugal, increases air pressure in several "stages". Part of the turbine then recovers energy from the hot gases to drive the compressor via a central shaft. The whole assembly forms one or more independent "spools", e.g. low and high pressure; some engines have three for greater flexibility. If the compressor is pushed too hard, the flow stalls, known as surge: sensors and ECUs prevent this by controlling valves and adjustable blades. Turbine blades, cut from nickel superalloys and sometimes monocrystalline, are pierced by tiny channels of cold air to prevent them from melting; a ceramic coating protects them. Sensors monitor temperature and vibration to keep a margin. All this mechanics serves a clear purpose: to obtain steady, reliable thrust, responsive to the pilot's commands.

The "pure" turbojet engine mainly accelerates the hot flow. Its signature is a relatively narrow nozzle and, often in military use, an afterburner that injects fuel after the turbine for extra thrust. This is perfect for short take-offs with heavy aircraft, or for getting past Mach 1, but it consumes a lot of fuel. At high speeds, the air intake becomes a crucial element: shock waves must be precisely positioned to slow the air down without chaos; ramp or mobile cone intakes take care of this. The pure jet therefore remains the tool of very fast aircraft, whether for hunting or research. In subsonic cruising, it is noisier and less economical than a blower, because it moves very little air very quickly. When speed is more important than economy, a compact, hot-core turbojet engine is ready to respond, with its lively thrust and airframe designed for supersonic aerodynamics.

The turboprop converts turbine energy into propeller drive. A reduction gearbox slows rotation so that the blades "bite" the air without approaching sonic speeds. The variable-pitch blades adapt the angle to each phase: small pitch to accelerate, large pitch to cross, feathering in the event of a breakdown to reduce drag, and inverted pitch on the ground to brake. At around 300 to 650 km/h, its propulsive efficiency is excellent, ideal for short runways, regional routes, mountainous missions or gravel operations. Modern blades, often scythe-shaped composites, reduce noise and vibration. The limits are mainly to be found at the tip of the blade: beyond this point, efficiency drops and noise rises. A turboprop therefore likes medium altitudes and moderate speeds, with outstanding take-off performance. Its winning recipe is simple: lots of gently accelerated air, little fuel, and precise control of torque and rpm.

The turbofan places a large shrouded propeller at the front, driven by the hot core. Some of the air bypasses the turbine: this is the "cold flow". The ratio of cold flow to hot flow is called the dilution ratio. The higher the dilution ratio, the more thrust comes from cold air, so the better for noise and fuel consumption in subsonic flight. Large aircraft use high dilution ratio fans, recognizable by their wide nacelles and acoustic chevrons or liners. Recent designs add a gearbox between fan and core: the "geared fan" provides a large, slower-running, even more efficient impeller. At the other end of the scale, low-dilution blowers are still useful when a fast, compact cell is required. In the future, open-rotor concepts, i.e. highly advanced propellers without full fairings, are looking for further gains, while maintaining noise levels compatible with airports.

On a day-to-day basis, these engines obey electronic brains called FADECs, which manage fuel, temperatures and limits. Start-up is by starter motor or APU, which rotates the core before ignition. During operation, torque, rpm, gas temperature (EGT) and vibration are monitored; a healthy EGT margin indicates a fit engine. Turboprops also require monitoring of pitch, blade symmetry and icing protection. All of them fear ingestions: gravel, birds or objects on the ground, hence the need for cautious procedures and safety cones. On the maintenance side, endoscopic scans inspect blades and chambers, oil analyses reveal wear and tear, and engine trends help to replace parts before they break down. Well piloted, well maintained, a turbojet, turboprop or fan becomes a faithful partner, transforming kerosene into useful kilometers with fascinating, reliable precision.

9.3 - Digital avionics, autopilot and fly-by-wire

In a modern cockpit, digital avionics replace isolated dials with screens that bring together the essentials. Two main screens tell the story of the flight: the PFD displays attitude, speed, altitude and flight director; the ND shows route, beacons and weather. A management computer, the FMS, calculates trajectory, fuel and time by linking GPS points, VORs and approach aids. Specialized computers (air, inertial and radio data) exchange data via standardized "buses", a bit like digital roads. Organized alerts (EICAS or ECAM) classify failures and procedures. Aids reinforce situational awareness: moving cartography, on-board weather, collision avoidance systems (TCAS) and ground proximity warning systems (EGPWS). This architecture is based on a simple idea: provide the right information, at the right time, using clear symbols. The pilot remains the decision-maker, but dialogues with systems that compare and cross-reference sensors, prevent errors and transform scattered data into a readable picture.

The sensors are the aircraft's "senses". The pitot-static system measures speed and altitude; an air-data computer corrects temperature and compressibility. Inertial units detect acceleration and rotation; GPS gives latitude, longitude and ground speed; a modern AHRS merges gyroscopes and accelerometers to display a stable horizon. The FMS cross-references everything: if the GPS falters, the inertial holds; if a probe becomes obstructed, a backup source takes over. Crews monitor this fusion with coherent indicators: speed scale with colored "ribbons", digital altitude, magnetic heading, estimated wind. Some cabins add synthetic vision and HUD to maintain a highly legible artificial horizon at night or in fog. On every flight, one rule remains: if a piece of information goes "off the rails", we compare sources, isolate the dubious, then follow the procedure. Robustness comes as much from redundancy as from careful cross-checking.

The autopilot is not a replacement pilot; it's a very precise arm. It controls servomotors on the control surfaces according to "modes". In roll, it can hold a heading (HDG) or follow an LNAV course; in pitch, it maintains an altitude, a vertical speed or a VNAV profile calculated by the FMS. An autothrottle adjusts engine speed to maintain a target speed. The flight director then traces two bars, which are centered on the stick if you're flying by hand. On approach, the aircraft captures a localizer and an ILS slope; on certified aircraft, the autoland guides you to touchdown in very low visibility. All this requires "mode awareness": knowing which mode is active, what it will do next, and when it will change. A good reflex is to announce important modes aloud, check the displayed target and take over as soon as any doubt arises. The autopilot increases precision if you keep a close eye on it.

Fly-by-wire replaces cables with sensors and computers that translate the pilot's gestures into commands for the actuators. The advantage is twofold: precision and protection. Pilot laws" limit angle of attack, load factor or excessive bank; the computer adds stability if the aircraft is naturally "lively", and compensates for attitude when thrust changes. The control stick can be a mini-side stick; it sends rate commands rather than direct positions, making the response uniform. If sensors fail, simpler folding laws take over, up to a "direct" mode where the pilot doses without assistance. The benefits can be seen everywhere: less oscillation in turbulence, even rounding, effort relief thanks to the automatic trim, and "alleviation" functions that relieve the wing during a gust. The principle remains transparent to the student: the pilot controls the intention, the machine intelligently distributes the effort.

Safety comes from redundant architectures and rigorously certified software. Many critical functions are tripled or quadrupled, powered by separate electrical and hydraulic circuits. Continuous testing (BITE) monitors sensors, ECUs and actuators; in the event of deviation, a healthy channel maintains control and an alert guides the crew. Recorders (FDR, CVR) store parameters and audio to improve safety as experience is gained. Certification verifies hardware and software to exacting levels; companies supplement this with procedures, a minimum equipment list and planned maintenance. On the crew side, anomaly checklists structure the response to a message: identify, stabilize, execute. This engineering-operating chain explains recent reliability: millions of hours in which sensors, computers and humans monitor each other, to ensure that information remains accurate, action proportionate, and the margin always present.

The human being remains at the heart of the system. Automation is a relief, but it can be a surprise if we lose our awareness of trends. The recipe is well known: brief the trajectory and minima, announce changes, check targets and modes, and keep the order "pilot, navigate, communicate". The schools train pilots to "go back to basics": steer by hand regularly, maintain speed and heading without assistance, recognize a doubtful indication and put it aside. Progress continues: data links (CPDLC), ADS-B "in" monitoring, precise RNP guidance, smarter alerts and predictive maintenance. Yet the best innovation remains a calm gaze, simple words, and constant comparison of sources. Digital avionics, autopilot and fly-by-wire don't replace judgment; they amplify it. By learning their logic, a young pilot discovers a patient companion which, well used, makes every flight more precise, cleaner and, above all, safer.

9.4 - Special configurations and flying wings

A configuration is the way in which you assemble wings, tailplanes, engines and landing gear to obtain a specific behavior. Some aircraft stick to the classic wing + tail recipe, while others shake things up to increase lift, range or stealth. We come across canards, delta wings, flying wings, V-shaped tailplanes, variable-geometry wings, pusher wings with a propeller at the rear, or even two-beam bimats. Behind these silhouettes lie simple equations: where the lift goes, how the drag closes, where the center of gravity is, and which control surface provides stability. A particular plan is never an aesthetic whim; it's a response to a mission: take off from a short runway, fly fast, glide far, reduce noise or carry a lot. To understand these choices is to read an aircraft as you would a well-thought-out tool: each curve tells the story of a compromise between efficiency, stability and ease of piloting.

The canard places a small wing in front of the main wing. The Wright brothers were already using a front plane as elevator. Later, Burt Rutan popularized the modern canard with his VariEze and Long-EZ, with tanks cleverly placed to maintain a healthy center of gravity. A well-tuned canard can stall first and "warn" the main wing, making behavior predictable. Larger aircraft have explored the formula, such as the composite Beech Starship and the Piaggio P.180 Avanti, recognizable by its propelling propellers and small noseplane. Close to the duck, the tandem wing distributes lift over two wings, like Henri Mignet's "Pou du Ciel", designed for simplicity. These families move the tail forward, freeing up the rear and reducing balancing drag. In return, they require a fine balance between surfaces, so that the flow from the first does not exhaust the next. The benefit comes when the coordination is right.

The delta wing, a wide, sturdy triangle, loves high speeds. Its large surface area and sharp leading edge create buoyant vortices at high incidence, useful for maneuvering and approach. Dassault made it famous with the Mirage; Convair explored it on the F-102 and F-106; Saab combined delta and canard on the Viggen, a recipe adopted by the Eurofighter Typhoon. A delta offers fuel volume, solid leading edge and structural simplicity, while remaining compatible with transonic profiles. Its historical shortcoming was a somewhat high approach speed; the addition of slats, flaps and sometimes a canard has made the formula smoother close to the ground. On the control side, elevons replace ailerons and elevator to manage roll and pitch without a tailplane. At high speed, the pronounced sweep reduces wave drag; at low speed, the hypersuspension devices boost lift. This triangular wing shows that a minimal design can serve demanding missions, from fast patrol to long-distance travel.

The flying wing removes the tail and keeps almost everything in the wing. The Horten brothers, Walter and Reimar, flew tailplaneless gliders; Northrop pursued the idea with the YB-35 and YB-49, then realized it decades later with the B-2 Spirit. The principle is appealing: no distinctive fuselage, less drag and a large internal volume for fuel. The control surfaces become elevons and yaw brakes, split to turn without vertical drift. The difficulty lies in stability: without a tail, the pitching return moment is low, and the wing must carry while controlling itself. Modern calculators and fly-by-wire help to maintain a clean attitude, making the formula viable on large aircraft. Blended wing body" demonstrators, such as the X-48, have explored wing-fuselage fusion in transport. Fewer protruding parts also mean a reduced radar signature. Here, purity of line is as much a question of aerodynamics as of discretion.

Changing the wing in flight offers other answers. The variable-geometry wing pivots to be very swept at high speed and more open at low speed. Aircraft such as the F-111, F-14, Tornado or B-1 have used this mechanism to reconcile short take-off and fast cruise, while accepting the mechanical complexity. Two experimental approaches have left their mark on engineering. The slanted wing of the AD-1 demonstrator pivoted in one piece to reduce transonic drag, validating the idea at low speeds. The Grumman X-29's inverted-swept wing exploited oriented carbon fibers and control laws to contain torsion and delay wingtip stall. This research shows how modern materials and electrical controls make possible geometries that were once untenable. The heart of the matter remains aeroelasticity: a flexible wing will twist; if we can control this torsion, we gain useful lift and fine control, without paying too much in weight.

Other special configurations focus on the tail. The V-tail, as on some versions of the Beechcraft Bonanza, combines fin and elevator in two inclined surfaces, gaining in drag but requiring clearly differentiated controls. The T-tail, common on DC-9s and CRJs, takes the elevator out of the engine's blast, but means you have to watch out for stalls at high incidence. Twin-beam bimats, seen on the P-38 Lightning and many UAVs, free up a rear ramp and simplify propeller installation. STOL aircraft such as the Fieseler Storch, DHC-6 Twin Otter or Pilatus PC-6 rely on large flaps, slats and a generous wing for short landings. Pusher propulsion systems, such as the Piaggio P.180, keep the noise out of the cabin and the wing clean. Each example reminds us that the aircraft is a sum of reasoned choices: when mission, materials and controls align, an original shape becomes an effective solution.

9.5 - Noise reduction and energy efficiency

Reducing noise and consuming less fuel often go hand in hand, because moving air efficiently requires less energy and generates a smoother flow. Aircraft noise comes from three main sources: the engine jet, the nose fan and the airframe itself (landing gear, flaps, leading edges). Authorities measure this noise in decibels according to published rules, and airports impose flight paths or time slots to protect local residents. As far as fuel is concerned, every kilo saved reduces weight, and therefore thrust, and therefore noise for the same amount of power. Engineers work on aerodynamics, engines and procedures; crews on take-off, descent and taxiing. When everything lines up, you get shorter take-offs, smoother climbs, smoother approaches and lower fuel consumption. For a young reader, remember the key idea: less turbulence and unnecessary speed means less noise and more kilometers flown for the same amount of fuel.

Modern engines reduce noise first and foremost by moving a lot of air slowly. A large fan at the front, typical of turbojet engines with high bypass ratios, produces most of the thrust with a quieter "cold flow". Acoustic liners line the nacelles to absorb certain frequencies, while herringbone cut-outs at the edge of the nozzle more gradually mix the hot jet with the ambient air. Fan blades, often made of composite, are thin, slightly twisted and sometimes fewer in number to limit noise interaction; their top speed is controlled to avoid approaching the rpm where noise climbs. ECUs manage ignition, fuel flow and limits to stay within the efficient zone. Maintenance also helps: a clean compressor, correct blade clearances and careful alignment maintain efficiency and reduce unnecessary blow-by. As a result, better-utilized thrust means a quieter sound and more kilometers saved.

The airframe, too, can whisper instead of hiss. On approach, airframe noise comes mainly from the flaps, slats and landing gear. Fairings smooth out the fasteners, covers and brushes limit vortices on the gear struts, and neat lips on the flaps reduce whistling. But steering is just as important as design. Continuous descent arrivals avoid abrupt landings and power overshoots; RNAV trajectories provide precise guidance for flying over fewer dwellings; airspeeds are kept measured so that flaps and gear are extended at the right moment, neither too early nor too late. On take-off, noise reduction procedures determine when to reduce thrust and at what speed to retract flaps. The objective remains the same: to remain stable, centred on the axis, and to transform the altitude lost or gained into a fluid trajectory. To the ear as to fuel flow, smoothness always pays off.

Fuel efficiency starts with drag. Wing-tip devices, called winglets or sharklets, recuperate some of the energy lost in wingtip vortices; from a distance, they can be recognized by their raised tips. Careful profiles and clean surfaces keep a boundary layer bonded for longer; a crushed insect on the leading edge is sometimes enough to degrade the finesse of a small aircraft, hence the importance of cleaning. Structures lightened by composites, honeycombs and titanium save hundreds of kilos on a fleet, reducing the amount of thrust required. Shrouded undercarriages, well-integrated antennas and closed joints add up to small gains that become big ones at the end of the year. In operation, choosing an altitude where the wind carries, planning step climbs as the aircraft becomes lighter, and avoiding unnecessary detours all improve the balance. Less drag and less weight is the simplest recipe for saving fuel.

Operational gestures complete the technique. On the ground, plugging in a fixed power supply and preconditioned air turns off the APU, a greedy and noisy little turbine. Single-engine taxiing when authorized, well-coordinated push-back tractors and short circuits limit unnecessary consumption. In flight, an economic index in the FMS helps to choose the speed that balances time and fuel costs; maintaining a clean configuration, avoiding prolonged airbrakes and anticipating descents saves precious kilos. Maintenance also contributes: washing the compressor, checking tire pressures, fine-tuning cooling flaps and replacing worn parts at the right time all help to maintain efficiency. Even cabin weight counts: adjusted drinking water quantities, optimized equipment and electronic documentation replace kilos of paper. Every little saving may seem modest, but over thousands of cycles, it makes a big difference, both to the ear and to the planet.

Sustainable aviation fuels, compatible with today's engines, reduce the carbon footprint over their entire life cycle when properly produced and tracked. They don't invent a magic silence, but can be integrated into the same aircraft and procedures to reduce overall impact. Around airports, noise abatement plans distribute take-offs and monitor measured levels; acoustic barriers protect the neighbourhood during engine tests; preferential schedules and runways avoid the most sensitive areas. The key is cooperation: engineers who design, mechanics who maintain, controllers who sequence, crews who apply, and local residents who provide useful feedback. Together, they transform a powerful machine into a more discreet neighbor and a more sober journey. Understanding the link between noise and efficiency means learning to look for a clean flow, a simple trajectory and a measured gesture. This patient search makes flights smoother, calmer and more economical, without losing the magic of the sky.

Chapter 10: Personalities and Great Aerial Exploits

10.1 - Louis Blériot and the English Channel 1909

In the summer of 1909, a London newspaper, the Daily Mail, promised a thousand pounds to anyone who could cross the English Channel in an aeroplane. The challenge seemed crazy, but Louis Blériot prepared methodically. For years, he had been breaking, repairing and improving. His Blériot XI, a simple, slender monoplane, seemed ready. Opposite him, Hubert Latham, the elegant pilot of the Antoinette, had already attempted the crossing and had to ditch after a breakdown. On July 25, near Calais, at the clairière des Baraques, the sea was gray and the wind capricious. Blériot, his leg bandaged after a recent burn, hobbled around his aircraft. Just after 4 a.m., he decides to set off in spite of the clouds. His crew tightened the shrouds, checked the 25-hp Anzani and filled the fuel tank. A French torpedo boat, the Escopette, served as a marker. The atmosphere is both simple and heroic: no radio, few instruments, just a compass and a lot of determination to turn a newspaper page into reality.

The Blériot XI is the epitome of lightweight ingenuity. Ash and poplar wood structure, varnished canvas canvas covering, slender wingspan of almost eight meters, frail but supple nosewheel. The fan-shaped three-cylinder Anzani engine makes the wooden propeller vibrate, biting into the cold morning air. Empty, the plane weighs just over two hundred kilos; with pilot and fuel, every kilogram counts. Blériot chose the monoplane for its finesse and low drag, when so many others swore by the biplane. He carried a small compass and relied on the sight of the torpedo boat to keep him on course. His plan was clear: take off early, stay low enough to avoid strong winds, correct the drift, then look for the white cliffs of England. This apparent simplicity conceals hours of testing. Every bolt, every wing strap has been designed to give the XI just one decisive quality: endurance just long enough.

Take-off takes place at around 4.41am. The plane tears itself away from the grassy field, leaps over the ruts, then levels out over a sea that breathes in long swells. The sound of the Anzani punctuates the minutes. There are no approach lights or beacons, only the wake of the Escopette and the occasional break in the mist. The crosswind gently pushed the aircraft eastwards; Blériot corrected on the control stick, played with the incidence, kept his concentration on the compass needle. Speed was modest, around seventy kilometers per hour; the distance, just under forty kilometers, seemed immense at this height. Thirty minutes pass. Suddenly, a white line appears in the darkness: the cliffs of Dover. Relief, but no let-up. We still had to choose a field, judge the slope and save our energy for the flare. The little monoplane held; it was up to the pilot to finish the line cleanly drawn in the air.

At around 5.17 a.m., Blériot landed near Dover Castle, at Northfall Meadow. The landing was firm, the nosewheel collapsed, but the main thing was there: the English Channel had been crossed in around thirty minutes. Witnesses rushed over, stunned. Journalists telegraphed the news, and the Daily Mail announced the victory and the reward. The unfortunate rival, Hubert Latham, sportsingly salutes the feat. Beyond the famous photo of Blériot smiling, cap in hand, the technical significance was immense: a light monoplane with a modest engine had linked two countries separated by the sea. Suddenly, a well-prepared airplane is no match for a liquid border. England, long protected by water, discovered that the sky ignores natural barriers. The crossing was not a stroll, but a disciplined flight, where every degree of heading and every engine revolution really counted.

The echo goes beyond the sporting feat. Staff and engineers understood that an aeroplane could cross an arm of the sea and deliver a message, a plan or a fresh perspective. Aircraft manufacturers drew inspiration from the XI to refine their monoplane designs, while navigation and engine reliability became priorities. A few weeks later, in Reims, the Great Aviation Week saw records soar. British pilots, hitherto cautious, threw themselves into local design and urged the government to invest. Blériot turned his success into a school and a business: he sold XIs, trained pilots and took part in airshows. Airfoils were adjusted, landing gear strengthened and minimal instrumentation standardized. The English Channel became a symbol: the airplane was no longer an improved kite, but a vehicle capable of regular service. A new page was turned, when the air became a space for thoughtful travel.

The Blériot XI of the crossing is today preserved at the Musée des Arts et Métiers in Paris, a tangible memory of a cool morning when a 25-horsepower engine was enough to change the scale of maps. His lesson goes beyond legend. It says that progress comes from a series of trials, corrected failures and lucid piloting. It also says that good preparation reduces chance: a simple compass, a floating marker, a controlled weight, a steady course. Finally, it shows that useful daring is not reckless. Blériot didn't go for it; he chose his time, his weather, his trajectory, and accepted a rough landing rather than a long approach. For a young reader, this story is not just a historic achievement. It's an instruction manual: observe, prepare, execute calmly. In this way, an entire sea becomes a flight corridor, and a reasonable dream, a possible route.

10.2 - Charles Lindbergh and the Atlantic 1927

In the mid-1920s, a New York hotelier offered the Orteig Prize to anyone who could fly non-stop between New York and Paris. Several teams attempt the adventure with multiple crews; none succeeds. A young airmail pilot, Charles Lindbergh, wants to attempt the feat solo. Supporters in St. Louis finance a custom-built aircraft, hence the name Spirit of St. Louis. The Ryan company in San Diego designed and built the airplane in just a few weeks, focusing on simplicity, lightness and endurance. Lindbergh's plan was clear: leave Long Island, aim for Newfoundland, cross the North Atlantic by dead reckoning, then seek out Ireland, England, the English Channel and Paris. No radio on board, just compass, turn indicator, clock, map and trained senses. The stakes were higher than financial reward: the aim was to prove that a well-prepared single-engine aircraft could cross an ocean and link two continents through the discipline of flight alone.

The Spirit of St. Louis is a high-wing monoplane, christened the Ryan NYP. Its heart is a Wright J-5C Whirlwind engine, radial, 9 cylinders, about 223 horsepower, reputedly reliable and air-cooled. For greater autonomy, the aircraft carries nearly 450 gallons of fuel in tanks positioned in front of the pilot, improving the balance and protecting the cabin. Frontal visibility is sacrificed for the tank; Lindbergh looks out through side windows and a periscope. No superfluous items: no upholstered seat, no heavy radio, minimal instrumentation, robust architecture. The wings carry simple shrouds, the wooden propeller translates energy without excessive vibration. Every kilogram saved becomes minutes of flight gained. The plane isn't fast, but it knows how to last. This engineering choice conveys an essential idea for long-distance flying: reliability, endurance, stability and rigorous navigation are better than useless top speed over an ocean.

At dawn on May 20, 1927, the plane took off from Roosevelt Field, a grassy runway weighed down by rain. Fully loaded, it ran for a long time, barely lifted off, skimmed the wires and slowly gained altitude. Heading northeast, Lindbergh skirted the coast to Newfoundland, battling fog, drizzle and cloud layers. To keep a reliable horizon, he sometimes descended very low, above the waves, then climbed again as soon as visibility improved. Navigation is by dead reckoning: compass course, speed, drift corrected by observing swell crests and ship smoke. At times, frost threatens, clouds close in, and the plane dances in cold gusts. Lindbergh notes his times, compares the angle of the sun, looks for alignments. The engine purrs regularly, proof that the mechanical preparation is paying off. Every hour passed reinforces a calm conviction: if discipline holds, the Atlantic can be reduced to a series of reasonable segments.

Fatigue becomes the main adversary. Postal nights have trained Lindbergh, but thirty hours of continuous attention require simple tricks: fresh air on the face, regular movements, small meals, measured water. Through a gap, stars confirm the course; in the morning, the light reveals a green and grey line on the horizon. This is Ireland. Satisfaction remains sober: we still have to skirt Great Britain, cross the English Channel and find the right terrain. The charts and coastal markers help; the weather improves at times, then closes in sheets. The Spirit remains stable, the engine steady. As Europe passes by, energy returns, buoyed by the closeness of the goal. The Channel is no longer Blériot's great leap, but a final march towards Paris. The flight, which began as a methodical gamble, took on the appearance of a demonstration: a well-thought-out itinerary, a simple machine, piloting that spared every gesture.

On the evening of May 21, Lindbergh reached the skies over Paris. The headlights of the cars traced serpentines around a black field, Le Bourget, where a huge crowd awaited the familiar silhouette. After a flight of 33 and a half hours, covering almost 5,800 kilometers, the

Spirit lands, rolls and comes to a halt with a bang. Witnesses swarmed the runway, carrying the pilot and telegraphing the news. The Orteig prize was won, but the real effect was greater: for the first time, a single man had flown non-stop between New York and Paris, in a single-engine plane, with controlled navigation and a sober engine. In the days that followed, Europe and America celebrated the feat. Beyond the images, a technical fact becomes clear: a well-designed, correctly loaded and methodically piloted aircraft can cross an ocean and arrive on schedule. The long distance changes scale, and the sky suddenly seems smaller.

The legacy of 1927 can be seen in the years that follow. Public confidence climbed, postal lines lengthened, airports were equipped and navigation training became more advanced. Engineers favored clean monoplane designs, long-lasting engines, well-placed fuel tanks and better instrumented cabins. Companies worked on weather, radio beacons and regularity, because magic had to become method. Schools took up the Lindbergh lesson for their pupils: prepare, lighten, check, hold your course, adapt without haste. The Spirit of St. Louis, preserved today in Washington, reminds us that a feat is not a stroke of luck. It's the sum of logical design, reliable mechanics and patient piloting. For you, the reader, this crossing is not just a beautiful story; it's an unobtrusive instruction manual for big business: transforming a line on a map into a real trajectory, held, and ultimately shared by all.

10.3 - Amelia Earhart and her daring crossings

In the 1920s and 1930s, Amelia Earhart embodied a new approach to air travel: scientific, methodical and curious. She first learned mechanics and navigation, then obtained her bachelor's degree and explored possible routes with an engineer's rigor. Each project follows the same recipe: choose the right aircraft, lighten the load, establish a trajectory and allow for margins. She takes precise notes on fuel consumption, weather and coastal landmarks, and talks to meteorologists and mechanics. Her ambition is not just to beat a time; she wants to show that disciplined piloting makes long crossings accessible aboard reasonable aircraft. She writes, lectures and encourages young people to learn. Her way of telling the story of the sky is simple: a sum of small decisions well taken. This attitude has led her to many famous challenges, where a reliable engine, a well-prepared airframe and a clear plan are better than risky bets. It's this method that makes her crossings daring and, above all, reproducible.

Her first Atlantic crossing, in 1928, was aboard a three-engine Fokker nicknamed Friendship. She was not at the controls, but worked on board as a crew member, observing the weather, taking readings, keeping the logbook and making joint decisions with the pilots. The success attracts public attention and proves that a transoceanic route is feasible when weather, fuel and navigation are prepared seriously. Earhart, grateful to the team, learns a lesson above all: the next step is to fly the aircraft herself, with a lighter machine and tighter navigation. She studied the charts from Newfoundland to Ireland, analyzed the prevailing winds, checked the necessary range and practiced fatigue management. The selection of the aircraft became crucial: a sturdy, economical single-engine plane capable of long cruises without overheating. Few announcements, lots of work behind the scenes. The maturing project was not an improvised stunt: it was a carefully framed experiment, ready to be tried solo.

In May 1932, she took off from Harbour Grace, Newfoundland, flying a carefully prepared red Lockheed Vega 5B. On board, simple but reliable instruments, a compass, gyros, gauges guarded like treasures, and fuel distributed to keep an honest balance. The plan is straightforward: heading east, moderate altitude to avoid the jet, drift corrected by judging on swells and clearings. The weather complicates the picture with frost and erratic rain, and fatigue sets in. Earhart holds the trim, adjusts the mixture, notes his times, compares positions and landmarks. After about fifteen hours, a green stripe appears: Ireland. She finally landed in Northern Ireland, proving that a single pilot, on a reasonable single-engine plane, can cross the Atlantic if the preparation holds. This flight confirmed an essential idea for the time: endurance, sky-reading and consistency on the stick counted as much as raw power. The new air routes gained a very concrete argument.

She continued in 1935 with a spectacular crossing between Hawaii and California, from Wheeler Field to Oakland, some 3,800 kilometers of Pacific solo. The heavy take-off requires a long runway and an engine monitored to the degree. Once cruising, the Pacific requires patient navigation: compass heading, estimated drift, scrupulous control of reserves. The landing in Oakland confirms the reliability of the plan and the aircraft. A few weeks later, she flew from Los Angeles to Mexico City, then from Mexico City to Newark in record time for the time, demonstrating that the same aircraft can fly very different profiles if weight, altitude and speed are adapted. Each flight became an applied study: weather, winds, fuel consumption, course-keeping. The newspapers speak of audacity; their readers discover above all a method. By linking far-flung cities, Earhart showed that aviation was not just a succession of feats, but an organized means of joining continents.

Above and beyond records, Earhart placed a central role in transmission. She wrote clear books, campaigned for the training of young people and co-founded an association of women pilots, the Ninety-Nines, created to help each other, share advice and improve safety. She insists on preparation: learning about the weather, respecting personal limits, taking care with weight and balance, and constantly checking her instruments. Her briefing style is concrete: trajectory, decision points, credible clearances. In public, she defends a useful and inclusive aviation style, where method prevails over the spectacular. The workshops she visits appreciate her technical curiosity; the schools, her way of encouraging realistic projects. This spirit attracts readers and students to aviation, where they finally see a place for themselves alongside engines and maps. His legacy gives crossings an educational dimension: the feat is not an isolated peak, but a trail for other crews to follow.

From his daring crossings, we learn a very practical lesson. A great journey is not an improvised feat, but a series of modest steps, each one validated before the next. Choose a simple, durable aircraft, lighten everything that can be lightened, prepare the route, monitor the weather and fuel, keep a watchful eye on exhaust points, then pilot cleanly and calmly. This framework makes it possible to deal with surprises without getting lost. Earhart adds a precious quality: curiosity, which leads to understanding mechanics, clouds and navigation rather than enduring them. A young reader can apply these ideas elsewhere than in the cockpit: for a homework assignment, for a sports project, for a team trip. You set a course, prepare your resources, check and adjust, and tell what you've learned. This is how a reasonable dream changes scale and becomes a safe route, ready to be taken by others.

10.4 - Jean Mermoz and Antoine de Saint-Exupéry

At the end of the First World War, an ambitious idea takes shape in Toulouse: to fly mail, quickly and regularly, from France to Morocco, then on to West Africa and South America. Pierre-Georges Latécoère launched the first lines, Didier Daurat imposed firm discipline, and a generation of pilots transformed the experiment. Among them, Jean Mermoz and Antoine de Saint-Exupéry became major figures. Their playground was by no means a tranquil circuit: the Sahara, the Atlantic and the Andes forced them to invent new methods. The planes, made of wood and canvas, then metal, flew with few instruments: compass, altimeter, watch, sometimes direction finder. Crews learned the weather by walking, reading dunes like maps and spotting breezes in the clouds. Each mailbag delivered on time strengthened the confidence of the linked towns. Little by little, air travel ceased to be a curiosity and became a reliable service, because pilots were able to turn risk into procedure.

Mermoz impressed first and foremost with his technical mastery and composure. On the Toulouse-Casablanca-Dakar route, he faced coastal fog, sandy winds and rudimentary runways. His recipe can be summed up in three words: prepare, check and decide. Preparing means knowing the weight and center of gravity, real range, alternate route and weather forecast for the hours ahead. Checking means following instruments and landmarks, comparing compass and felt course, keeping the ball centered even in choppy air. Deciding means giving up if the margin shrinks, or taking advantage of a short window of opportunity to cross a pass, a layer or a front. In the desert, you need to be sure of what you're doing: spot lines of dunes to estimate drift, choose a clean axis away from mirages, save your machine. Several times, breakdowns force him to land in the sand and repair on the spot with the help of mechanics or patrols. These episodes became lessons that sharpened the line and simplified procedures.

On May 12, 1930, Mermoz opened the South Atlantic mail route between Saint-Louis in Senegal and Natal in Brazil. Aboard a floatplane Laté 28-3, he surrounded himself with a navigator, Jean Dabry, and a radio operator, Léopold Gimié. Preparations were meticulous: fuel weighed, engine tested at a fixed point, route calculated with expected winds, plans for retreat to the Fernando de Noronha archipelago. Night and day, the flight relies on constant heading and the quality of radio messages. Above a seemingly motionless ocean, the crew watches for cross swells and clouds to correct the drift. The crossing lasts over twenty hours, at a modest but steady speed. When the coast of Brazil appears, it's less a triumph than a technical validation: the aeropostale can cross the sea, provided that weight, weather and method are respected. This success paved the way for larger seaplanes, better-trained crews and weekly connections.

Saint-Exupéry built his reputation both in the desert and in South America. As airfield manager at Cap Juby, on the Sahara coast, he organized rescues and negotiations to recover crews stranded far from the roads, improved the radio and established routines that calmed emergencies. Later, in Argentina, he took part in the Aeroposta project, scouting the terrain, installing beacons and setting up Andean refuges for difficult weather crossings. With companions like Henri Guillaumet, he learned to read the Andes: gliding downwind of ridges, monitoring the formation of lenticulars, setting safety altitudes and turning points. His piloting is precise, energy-efficient and attentive to both the aircraft and the air. Above all, he keeps logbooks in which every flight becomes an experience report: actual fuel consumption, practicable corridors, terrain traps. This shared memory enhances the safety of the entire line.

Aéropostale became a laboratory for still-familiar methods. Structured briefings, concise phraseology, planned maintenance and cartography that was useful to the pilot, not decorative, were born. Radio beacons and direction-finding reduced deviations, night navigation was based on a sequence of lights and limited headings, and minimum sector altitudes were set for avoiding masked terrain. Line managers imposed checklists and progress reports, while mechanics perfected engines and propellers to save minutes and increase reliability. Trajectories are smoothed out: unnecessary landings are avoided, descent is anticipated, and a stable approach speed is maintained. Each incident becomes a record, each record an improvement. This patient weaving transforms an isolated exploit into a mastered routine. A regular airmail service can only exist if a thousand small details are agreed, from the weather schedule to the tools in the toolbox.

Their heritage lies in a simple ethic, useful to all pilots. Respecting the machine and the sky, preferring method to bravery, transforming a risk into a plan, a doubt into verification. Mermoz and Saint-Exupéry proved that a long flight is nothing more than a series of short, well-prepared and well-kept segments, and that a map filled with emptiness can be read if reliable landmarks are placed on it. They have shown that you can cooperate with mechanics, radios, meteorologists and local authorities to create a line where there was only a pencil line. Today's major roads owe them their reflexes: clear briefings, clean radios, safe altitudes, timely decisions. At the age of twelve or seventeen, we can already draw inspiration from them: choose a reasonable course, prepare our means, keep a margin, and move forward step by step. This is how the cards are opened up and dreams become sure paths.

10.5 - Concorde and the civil supersonic era

In the 1960s, France and the UK decided to build a faster-than-sound airliner together. The project was given the ambitious name of Concorde, and brought two major industrialists together around the same roadmap. The engineers were looking for an aircraft capable of flying at Mach 2, i.e. twice the speed of sound, while carrying passengers like a conventional aircraft. The first prototype took off from Toulouse in 1969, proving in progressive tests that stable supersonic cruise flight was possible. After several years of tests, adaptations and international agreements, it entered service in 1976 with Air France and British Airways. Between Paris or London and New York, journey times were suddenly cut almost in half. More than just a record, Concorde was a technological demonstration: bringing together aerodynamics, engines and materials to create a supersonic civil aircraft that was safe, pilotable and capable of operating on regular routes.

To maintain Mach 2, Concorde adopted a thin, swept ogival delta wing, which remained efficient when the air was compressed. At high incidence, the leading edge generates buoyant vortices that maintain lift at low speeds, useful for take-off and landing. The fuselage is long and tapered to reduce wave drag. The nose can be tilted downwards on take-off and approach to improve pilot visibility, then raised again in cruise. In fast flight, aerodynamic heating expands the aluminum structure by a few centimeters; the designers provide joints and tolerances to keep everything snug. The tanks are distributed along the length of the fuselage, and also serve to shift the center of gravity by pumping in fuel according to the phase of flight. This geometry, combined with efficient controls and a light but rigid structure, transforms the engines' energy into a fine, stable and comfortable trajectory for passengers.

Propulsion is based on four Olympus 593 turbojet engines, designed by Rolls-Royce and Snecma, equipped with an afterburner for the take-off and acceleration phases. The variable-geometry air inlet is the real key: moving ramps position the shock waves to slow and compress the air before the compressor, protecting the engine and improving supersonic efficiency. At cruising altitude, Concorde flies at around 18,000 metres, at Mach 2, where cold, thin air reduces drag. Pilots follow temperature, rpm and pressure settings, supervised by dedicated computers that monitor intake and thrust. The sonic boom imposes routes over the ocean, as over land the wave would be a nuisance. This fine management of air, fuel and speed makes a very powerful engine a measured partner. The result is a sustained climb, followed by a very fast, stable and surprisingly regular cruise.

On a daily basis, the aircraft carries around a hundred passengers on a light, fast service, designed for three- to four-hour crossings between Europe and North America. Taxiing and take-off require a long runway and a precise sequence of flaps, thrust and rotation. Approach speeds are high by subsonic standards, requiring robust brakes and thrust reversers, as well as a large main gear. The cabin, pressurized and thermally insulated, remains comfortable despite the high altitude and lukewarm skin due to overheating. The choice of aluminum rather than titanium facilitates manufacturing and maintenance, while keeping weight under control. Crews rely on strict procedures, intake computers and avionics that simplify ocean navigation. From the passenger's point of view, the experience combines an energetic take-off, a sustained climb, a short, punctual cruise, then a continuous descent towards the opposite coast.

Why a small fleet and limited routes despite technical success? The answer lies in economics, noise and regulations. The oil crisis increased fuel costs, and supersonic flight consumes considerably more fuel than subsonic long-haul flights. The sonic boom prohibits most land overflights at Mach 2, limiting profitable ocean routes. Noise requirements for take-off and landing call for precise procedures and adapted airports. Despite these constraints, Concorde served for decades, proving that regular operation is possible when maintenance, training and planning are right. Above all, it leaves a legacy of engineering: controlled air intakes, ogival delta, fuel management for centering, multiple redundancies, and a very strict measurement culture. Many of its engineers and pilots went on to form the next generation of modern aircraft, in which the same obsession with precision and stability can be found.

Concorde closed its career in the early 2000s, having demonstrated that supersonic civil transport could operate on a daily basis on targeted routes. The era that followed favored sober, silent wide-body aircraft, but Concorde's imprint remains in engineering schools, test centers and simulators. It provided the tools to master shock waves, variable intake, thermal expansion and fine-tuned energy management. Other supersonic programs, such as the earlier Tupolev Tu-144, have explored different choices and nurtured the same quest for efficiency. Today, laboratories are studying bang reduction and aeroacoustics to make fast flights more discreet, while working on lower-carbon fuels. Without promising the future, we can read a lasting lesson: when the method meets audacity, an aircraft can move the boundaries of the possible, and then pass on its tools to the whole of civil aviation.

Conclusion

Page after page, you've followed the rise of flight, from ancient dreams to the first ascents, then from silent gliders to durable jet engines. You've seen how stubborn tests became methods, and how air routes linked continents. Each chapter has revealed a tool: understanding the air, reading the map, preparing, checking, deciding, then flying with accuracy.

You now know the forces that govern an airplane: lift, drag, weight and thrust. You know that a well-tuned airfoil, the right incidence and coordinated control surfaces turn the air into an ally. Instruments tell the story of vertical and attitude; weather, space and performance dictate margins. The navigation prepares the route, the checklist secures every gesture.

You met pilots, mechanics, controllers and instructors who share the same culture: briefing, communicating, cross-checking, respecting the flight envelope. Materials, engines and systems have shown that engineering wins when it remains humble and precise. This rigor takes nothing away from the beauty of the sky: it enables regular, safe travel, and calm decisions in the face of doubt.

The most important thing is to continue practicing curiosity and method. Watch the birds, read the clouds, measure before you act, then tell us what you've learned. Every step in this book can become a useful habit on the ground and in the air. Keep your mind clear, your eyes wide and your course simple: knowledge always opens the sky.

Frederick Jany

Quiz

1) Which ancient object directly illustrates Archimedes' thrust applied to air?
- a) The kite attributed to Mozi and Lu Ban
- b) Celestial lanterns associated with Zhuge Liang
- c) Heron of Alexandria's éolipile
- d) Archytas' mechanical pigeon

2) Which animals served as first passengers on a test flight by the Montgolfier brothers in 1783?
- a) A dog, a cat and a pigeon
- b) A sheep, a rooster and a duck
- c) Two goats and a goose
- d) A rabbit, a hawk and a tortoise

3) Which Wright brothers' innovation became the standard for flying an airplane?
- a) The ogival delta wing
- b) The three-axis control system (pitch, roll, yaw)
- c) cabin pressurization
- d) Jet propulsion

4) What control evolution replaced wing warping on the biplanes of 1908-1914?
- a) The addition of articulated ailerons
- b) Adoption of a V-shaped tail unit
- c) the installation of high lift flaps
- d) cabin pressurization

5) What does a glider's glide ratio of 30 mean?
- a) It travels 30 km, losing 1 km of altitude.
- b) Its minimum speed is 30 km/h
- c) Its optimum angle of attack is 30°.
- d) It can carry 30 kg of ballast

6) Which control on a helicopter changes the pitch of all the blades simultaneously to climb or descend?
- a) The cyclic stick
- b) Collective
- c) Tail pedals

d) Rotor pre-launch

7) In stabilized flight, which equalities correctly describe the balance of forces?
a) Lift > weight and thrust < drag
b) Lift = weight and thrust = drag
c) Lift &lgt; weight and thrust > drag
d) Lift = drag and weight = thrust

8) What effect does a higher load factor have on stall speed?
a) It decreases in proportion to the load factor
b) It increases, depending on the root of the load factor
c) It remains constant if trim is correctly set
d) Depends solely on wind and not on load factor

9) What altimeter setting is used above the transition altitude so that everyone reads the same altitude?
a) The QFE of the departure aerodrome
b) The regularly updated local QNH
c) The standard 1013 hPa (29.92 inHg) setting
d) A manual setting to display zero in level flight

10) What do the square numbers mean on a VFR chart?
a) The average magnetic variation of the area
b) Recommended cruising altitude
c) Highest obstacle in the quadrant concerned
d) QNH to be used for the flight

11) In Europe (EASA), what is the minimum age for a first solo glider flight?
a) 12 years old
b) 14 years old
c) 16 years old
d) 18 years old

12) After start-up, what parameter must rise within seconds to confirm engine health?
a) Exhaust gas temperature
b) Oil pressure
c) Battery voltage
d) Fuel flow

13) Which emblematic aircraft proved that it was possible to fly fast, far and at controlled cost, opening up stable networks?
   a)   de Havilland Comet
   b)   Douglas DC-3
   c)   Boeing 747
   d)   Farman F.40

14) Which document authorizes a flight with non-essential equipment temporarily unavailable, under certain conditions?
   a)   NOTAMs
   b)   MEL, minimum equipment list
   c)   Loadsheet
   d)   Arrival STAR

15) Which device extends the endurance of a fighter patrol according to the chapter?
   a)   Afterburner for more thrust
   b)   In-flight refueling
   c)   Winglets to reduce drag
   d)   Cabin pressurization to fly higher

16) Which drone sensor emits laser pulses to create a geo-referenced point cloud?
   a)   RGB camera
   b)   Thermal camera
   c)   LiDAR
   d)   A stabilized gimbal

17) In a "sandwich" structure, which element maintains the spacing of the skins and mainly takes up shear forces?
   a)   Composite skins
   b)   Honeycomb or foam core
   c)   Fastening rivets
   d)   Protective paint

18) Which configuration eliminates the tailplane and uses elevons and split yaw brakes for control?
   a)   The canard
   b)   The delta wing
   c)   The flying wing
   d)   The two-beam bimat

19) What was the main landmark that helped Blériot stay on course when crossing the English Channel in 1909?
   a)   The cliffs of Étretat
   b)   The French torpedo boat L'Escopette
   c)   A VOR radio beacon installed in Calais
   d)   An accompanying airship

20) Which archipelago was used as a fallback when Mermoz crossed the South Atlantic in 1930?
   a)   The Azores
   b)   Fernando de Noronha
   c)   Canary Islands
   d)   Cape Verde

Answers

1) Which ancient object directly illustrates Archimedes' buoyancy applied to air?

Correct answer: b) The celestial lanterns associated with Zhuge Liang.

2) Which animals served as first passengers on a test flight by the Montgolfier brothers in 1783?

Correct answer: b) A sheep, a rooster and a duck.

3) Which Wright brothers' innovation became the standard for flying an airplane?

Correct answer: b) The three-axis control system (pitch, roll, yaw).

4) What control evolution replaced wing warping on biplanes from 1908-1914?

Correct answer: a) The addition of articulated ailerons

5) What does a glide ratio of 30 mean for a glider?

Correct answer: a) It travels 30 km, losing 1 km in altitude.

6) Which control on a helicopter changes the pitch of all the blades simultaneously to climb or descend?

Correct answer: b) Collective

7) In stabilized flight, which equalities correctly describe the balance of forces?

Correct answer: b) Lift = weight and thrust = drag

8) What effect does a higher load factor have on stall speed?

Correct answer: b) It increases, depending on the root of the load factor.

9) What altimeter setting is used above the transition altitude so that everyone reads the same altitude?

Correct answer: c) The standard 1013 hPa (29.92 inHg) setting.

10) What do the square numbers mean on a VFR chart?

Correct answer: c) The highest obstacle in the quadrant concerned.

11) In Europe (EASA), what is the minimum age for a first solo glider flight?
Correct answer: b) 14 years

12) After start-up, what parameter must rise within seconds to confirm engine health?
Correct answer: b) Oil pressure

13) Which emblematic aircraft proved that it was possible to fly fast, far and at controlled cost, opening up stable networks?
Correct answer: b) Douglas DC-3

14) Which document authorizes a flight with non-essential equipment temporarily unavailable, under certain conditions?
Correct answer: b) MEL, minimum equipment list

15) Which device extends the endurance of a fighter patrol according to the chapter?
Correct answer: b) In-flight refueling

16) Which drone sensor emits laser pulses to create a georeferenced point cloud?
Correct answer: c) LiDAR

17) In a "sandwich" structure, which element keeps the skins apart and mainly takes up shear forces?
Correct answer: b) The honeycomb or foam core.

18) Which configuration eliminates the tailplane and uses elevons and split yaw brakes for control?
Correct answer: c) The flying wing

19) Which main landmark helped Blériot stay on course when crossing the English Channel in 1909?
Correct answer: b) The French torpedo boat L'Escopette

20) Which archipelago was used as a fallback plan when Mermoz crossed the South Atlantic in 1930?
Correct answer: b) Fernando de Noronha

Printed in Dunstable, United Kingdom

71501470R00080